"Cousin or Not . . . You're Insufferable!"

"I wouldn't cross the street to get your autograph," Deborah raged.

Clement merely threw back his head and laughed. When he finished he said, "Well? Answer my question. What *do* you want here?"

With more resolve than she felt, Deborah began. "I'm working on my master's degree in English, and I plan to write *The Personal Life of Clement Vaulkhurst.*"

In the silence that followed, his coal black eyes took on a harsh expression. In the next instant his deep baritone, barely audible, left little doubt of the listener's reaction.

"No little graduate student with no talent whatsoever is going to pry into *my* personal life."

PATTI BECKMAN'S
interesting locales and spirited characters will thoroughly delight her audience. She lives with her husband Charles and their young daughter on the gulf coast of Texas.

Dear Reader:

Silhouette Romances is an exciting new publishing venture. We will be presenting the very finest writers of contemporary romantic fiction as well as outstanding new talent in this field. It is our hope that our stories, our heroes and our heroines will give you, the reader, all you want from romantic fiction.

Also, *you* play an important part in our future plans for Silhouette Romances. We welcome any suggestions or comments on our books and I invite you to write to us at the address below.

So, enjoy this book and all the wonderful romances from Silhouette. They're for *you!*

Karen Solem
Editor-in-Chief
Silhouette Books
P. O. Box 769
New York, N.Y. 10019

PATTI BECKMAN
Angry Lover

Silhouette *Romance*

Published by Silhouette Books New York

America's Publisher of Contemporary Romance

For Sharla

Other Silhouette Romances by Patti Beckman

The Beachcomber
Captive Heart
Louisiana Lady

SILHOUETTE BOOKS, a Simon & Schuster Division of
GULF & WESTERN CORPORATION
1230 Avenue of the Americas, New York, N.Y. 10020

Copyright© 1981 by Patti Beckman

Distributed by Pocket Books

ISBN: 0-671-57072-2

First Silhouette printing April, 1981

10 9 8 7 6 5 4 3 2 1

America's Publisher of Contemporary Romance

Printed in the U.S.A.

Chapter One

Deborah clutched her glass tightly when she heard the name Clement Vaulkhurst. She had spent days rehearsing the speech she would give her mother after tonight's party, and the mere mention of the name Vaulkhurst set her nerves on edge. She chided herself for being such a weakling.

You can do it, she told herself firmly. There's not a reason in the world why you can't strike out on your own this summer and do the research for your thesis, just the way you've planned.

Deborah stood by the doorway lost in thought, surrounded by her parents' colleagues. Her mother and father were giving their annual spring faculty cocktail party at their campus home close to the small Connecticut university where they both taught. As usual, the conversation had gotten around to her eminent relative, Clement Vaulkhurst.

"I understand Clement Vaulkhurst is related to you, Dr. Denhoff."

Deborah's mother replied, "Yes, we are second cousins, although it is not a blood tie. My great-aunt adopted and raised him."

"How fascinating to have such a notable person in your family!"

"Notable . . . or notorious." Dr. Margaret Denhoff laughed wryly. "Cousin Clement has tweaked quite a few literary noses in his career."

Clement Vaulkhurst always provided the subject for a good hour's discussion at any party given by Deborah's parents. Not every person could lay claim to having a Nobel- and Pulitzer-prize–winning novelist as a distant relative, even if only an adopted one. A new faculty member, upon discovering the relationship, was usually intrigued and eager to hear, at first hand, family anecdotes about the renowned novelist. Later, those in the English department could pass the stories on to their classes, thereby gaining for themselves a certain name-dropping prestige.

"Cousin Clement is an enigma to the literary world," Dr. Denhoff continued. "Little has been written about him as a person. He's a great practical joker and completely unconcerned about what others think of him. He once told me quite seriously that he had been only a mediocre writer until he made a pact with the devil!"

There was a round of nervous laughter. The circle of faculty members surrounding Deborah's mother was growing larger. Soon, everyone in the room would be wedged into a tight corner with Dr. Denhoff, tossing out speculations about Clement Vaulkhurst and his writings. To them it was an amusing and intriguing intellectual game. But to Deborah Denhoff, the subject of Clement Vaulkhurst had come to signify a milestone in her life. She could not help being fascinated by his writing, and it was the pursuit of his work and the unraveling of the mystery of his private life that were going to free her.

Deborah's father moved through the crowded room in her direction, bearing a tray of hors d'oeuvres. "The little square ones aren't bad," he offered.

"I'll try one on your suggestion," Deborah said, making an effort to conceal her nervousness.

Dr. Foster Denhoff glanced toward his wife, who was surrounded by a circle of intense, bearded young faculty members.

"Cousin Clement?" he asked dryly.

Deborah nodded.

"Oh, well, it will give them some material for lectures in the English department this summer. The school once offered him a position as author in residence, you know."

"Cousin Clement?" she asked, somewhat surprised. "No, I didn't know. . . . These really are good. What are they?"

"A mixture of cheese and bacon, I think. . . . Yes, he turned it down, though. Sent a rather insulting letter of refusal to the president, as I recall."

Dr. Denhoff chuckled and Deborah smiled. But inwardly, she was clench-fisted over the confrontation she knew she must have with her parents after the party. When she broke the news of her plans for the summer it would certainly precipitate a family crisis, and she dreaded such things. It would not be any sort of shouting, emotional row; her parents were entirely too civilized for anything so gauche. But they would become cool, stiff, and disapproving with her, and she thought she'd really rather that they shouted.

She glanced up at her father. Up, because Foster Denhoff was a tall, spare man, six foot three. He had more of an outdoorsy, weather-beaten complexion than the usual college professor. That was a result of the summers he spent off in various jungles, poking about in archaeological ruins. In his late fifties, he was still a handsome figure of a man despite his hair that had thinned to a few remaining strands slicked across a shiny scalp. His clothes invariably had a slightly rumpled appearance, and he hadn't the vaguest notion what color necktie to wear. Nevertheless, every semester a number of freshman girls in his archaeology class fell desperately in love with him—a fact that would have astounded and horrified him had he ever been aware of it. Deborah didn't believe, however, that he was ever really conscious of any individuals in his classes. Students to him were not people so much as functional necessities to provide him with the opportunity to lecture on the absorbing passion of his life: archaeology.

A bushy-haired young man wearing horn-rimmed glasses was eagerly working his way through the guests toward Deborah. The clenched fist inside her tightened. Bill Hughbank. She had to cope with him today, too. First Bill, then her parents. She wasn't sure she was up to it.

"Hello, Dr. Denhoff."

"Bill." Her father nodded.

"Well, hi," he said to Deborah, a trifle breathless, as if he'd run the final block to her house.

"Well, hi," she said uncomfortably.

"Sorry I'm late. Had to finish packing and stop off at the book store. You know how it is at the end of semester, not to mention graduation."

"You didn't miss anything," she said.

Bill and her father were shaking hands, unaware of her irony.

"Well, I'm sure you two have a lot to talk about," Dr. Denhoff said and wandered off.

"Well, hi," Bill said, taking her hand.

"You already said that." Somewhat nervously, she got her hand back from him.

"Gee, we really do have a lot to talk about," Bill rushed on enthusiastically. "I mean, there are so many plans we have to make. I've been tied up with final exams and all, but now that that's over we can think about you and me."

She realized how tightly she was holding her empty glass and put it down. Bill's impetuous enthusiasm had once seemed attractive to her, probably because of her own lack of initiative. It had swept her right along with no effort on her part, like letting go and flowing downstream on a raft with her eyes closed. But now it was distracting. Suddenly, she found herself about to swim against the stream. Best to plunge right in before she lost her nerve.

"Bill, let's go for a ride. We can't talk here."

"Sure," he replied cheerfully.

She felt a pang. Bill was basically a nice person, and she didn't wish to hurt or disappoint him. But that's your problem, Deborah, she thought, or at least one of your problems. You've spent your life to this point trying to avoid hurting or disappointing anyone, or taking any chances, and it has gotten you where you are now—precisely nowhere.

They left the party and walked to Bill's late-model Chevrolet which was parked down the block. The winding, tree-fringed residential street here on faculty row was heavily parked with cars because of the party at her home.

As Bill drove to a quiet place where they could talk, Deborah tried to organize her thoughts. She'd known Bill now for two years. He was a thoroughly decent, respectable young man, entirely suitable husband material. He was studying law and would pass his bar examination this summer and go right into his father's law firm. There was nothing surprising or unsettling about Bill. He was a Young Republican, never got involved in campus demonstrations, didn't use drugs or have a drinking problem. A girl should count herself lucky indeed to be engaged to a stable young man like Bill who had such a promising future.

She bit at her fingernail. "Bill, I want to put off the engagement."

He had parked beside a small lake on the western rim of the campus. His blue eyes framed by dark, heavy-rimmed glasses were gazing at her fondly, and he was smiling.

"What?"

"The engagement. I don't want to get engaged this summer."

The smile began to fade. "But I thought it was all settled. We agreed—I mean, everything is set—"

"Could it get unset for a while?"

The blue eyes were frowning now. "I don't understand, Deborah."

She was getting that old, trapped, claustrophobic sensation. "I realize it's disappointing to you, Bill, but I want to—to postpone everything."

"Until when?"

"Well—next fall sometime," she hedged.

He was shaking his head with an expression of hurt confusion. She felt miserable but adamant.

"Can you give me one good reason why?"

"Well, for one thing, I plan to write my thesis this summer. It's all I lack now on my master's."

He looked relieved. "That's no problem. Getting engaged and married needn't interfere. . . ."

"It will. I want to have the degree first. It's important to me. Besides, you don't understand. I'm going to write the thesis on Clement Vaulkhurst. Dr. Groves in the English department has okayed it—"

Blue eyes frowning. Lips in a scowl. "Clement Vaulkhurst? The writer fellow in your family?"

"Distantly in my family: a second cousin, and an adopted one at that."

"I still don't see what all this has to do with us. Why can't we get married first, and then you can research this fellow or whatever it is you want to do."

She hesitated. Was she making a mistake? She searched the new *her* for an answer.

No, behind putting Bill off were all the old problems that he represented and that had kept her single until age twenty-four. She was a people pleaser. She had lived up to what she thought her parents had expected of her, and she had felt responsible for their happiness. As the youngest child in the family, she had not made a declaration of independence and left home for fear that her parents would feel alone and adrift with no more children with them. She had just lived through a year of sheer misery, and she was only now beginning to realize that it was all tied up with trying to do what other people expected of her, instead of doing what she wanted to do. Even Bill was part of that. Her parents found him stable, reliable, comfortable, just the kind of son-in-law they would like to have look after their not too capable daughter. But she sensed that somewhere in the depths of her being there was a capable, able woman waiting to be called on to perform tasks that she felt were important. Her parents wouldn't like her summer plans, and up until now she had never had the nerve to insist on doing what she wanted; but somehow, out of the depths of her despair over being suffocated by a life that she hadn't really chosen for herself, she was finding the fortitude to begin standing up for herself and to make the first attempts to demand what she wanted out of life.

While she tried to analyze her feelings and attempted to explain them to Bill, she found herself at last relying on her instinct. Marrying Bill, her better judgment told her, was wrong.

Was the decision based on not being entirely sure if she loved him? It was a question she wasn't ready to face, and she needed the summer to give her the time and perspective to know her own heart better.

She spent another half hour with Bill in the parked car, arguing, Bill going from persuasion to pleading. Finally, becoming a bit desperate, he resorted to basic physical appeal, and there was a lengthy, perspiring, clutching entanglement from which she finally emerged disheveled and even more convinced that she was not ready for marriage—at least not to Bill.

Finally, Bill took Deborah home, where she faced the unnerving prospect of confronting her parents with her summer plans. It would be another dreaded ordeal. Only her newly found resolve gave her the courage to go through with it.

Deborah entered the living room. The party was

over, and she saw the usual postparty clutter—glasses and ashtrays scattered about—that would remain until next morning when Grace, the maid, arrived. Her mother's response to any type of housekeeping situation was to look dismayed and retire to her study.

Deborah's parents had enjoyed a reasonably satisfactory thirty-year marriage, even though they were absorbed in their individual pursuits, her father as head of the university's archaeology department and her mother with her tenure in the psychology department. Every summer, her father went trekking off to poke around some old ruins for a couple of months while her mother worked on another paper in her field. The annual separation did not appear to bother them. They were so preoccupied with their pursuits that Deborah wasn't sure one noticed that the other was missing.

Deborah came from a family of eggheads. In her family, anyone who had not earned his or her doctorate by age twenty-six was suspected of being mentally retarded. Her sister, Jan, was head of a research department in oceanography at a West Coast university. Her brother, Phil, a nuclear physicist, was in the aerospace program at NASA. All except Deborah were members of Mensa, the club exclusively for persons with near-genius IQs.

She was the slow learner in the family. Courses that Jan and Phil flipped through required agonized digging for Deborah to make a passing C in them. She knew it was a source of embarrassment to her parents that, at age twenty-four, she was just finishing her master's degree, and, at that, her grade-point average was dismally low, just getting her by.

It wasn't until she had done some recent soul-searching that she finally realized she was just as

capable as anyone else in her family. Her low grades
were the result of trying to live out someone else's
expectations of her. She hadn't been suited for the life
she had tried to fit into, and she was beginning to rankle
just a bit at the thought of the time she had wasted.
Now she was going to do something she wanted to do.
It was becoming increasingly important to her to stand
up for her rights, hard as it might be after getting off to
such a late start in life doing it.

What she had in mind wasn't so much really, and yet
thoughts of telling her parents her plans made her grind
her teeth with apprehension. She had never gone
against their wishes. She had never made a major
decision without consulting them and then doing what
they wanted her to do. She steeled herself and left the
living room in search of her mother. She knew she must
do it now while she still had the nerve. What was the
matter with her, anyway? She was a grown woman. She
hardly had to ask permission for what she wanted to do,
she told herself. But in spite of her determination,
butterflies danced in her stomach.

She found her parents in the den. "I'd like to talk to
you," she said deliberately, in a voice she held under
control. "It's about the subject of my thesis."

"Oh?" her father said. "Have you made a decision?"

"Yes, I have. I want to write about Clement Vaulkhurst."

"Why, I think that's a splendid choice," her mother
exclaimed enthusiastically. But her enthusiasm faded
when Deborah went on to explain how she planned to
research her material.

"I want to spend the summer in Uromund, Texas,
where Clement lives."

Her mother frowned and adjusted her hearing aid. She was nearsighted and slightly hard of hearing. The sight of the hearing aid in her ear often caused her students to speak above normal volume, which was entirely unnecessary since she heard as well as anybody else so long as she used her aid. The device was well suited to her stiff, iron-gray hair, tweed suits, and rimless glasses, all of which lent her an air of imposing dignity. Like Deborah's father, she was tall, several inches above average height. Tallness along with high IQs ran in the family, except for Deborah. She was barely five foot two. She often joked about having a chronic stiff neck from looking up at her relatives.

"I fail to see any value in traipsing off to that awful place where Clement lives. It's a dreary, isolated town, and that house of his is practically in a swamp. You could do a much more valuable thesis about his writings."

Deborah shook her head. "I have in mind a biographical approach. So little is known about Clement Vaulkhurst himself. His personal life is a mystery. I'd like to find out about the man—what kind of person he really is. . . ."

Her father warned, "You may not like what you turn up. Clement is a strange man, not like other men. Many people dislike him because of his independence and arrogance. There may be things about his life better left uncovered."

Then her mother asked, "How about young Bill Hughbank? I thought the two of you might be planning a wedding this coming summer."

"That's been postponed."

There was an awkward silence. Deborah bit at her

fingernail. Her mother cleared her throat. "Clement is not going to appreciate your poking around in his private life. Being a distant relative will not make him any more civil to you. . . ."

Deborah tried to make them understand her position. She'd become convinced that one day she must make this break. The longer she waited, the more difficult it would be, until, if she waited too long, she'd become permanently dependent on her family or on Bill. That would be fine if she were ready to marry Bill. She was not a women's libber at heart. When she found her man and married, he would be the center of her universe. But she was not convinced Bill was right for her.

Now she had a purpose, a goal, something that at last she wanted to do on her own, away from the safe security of the university campus. The mystery about Clement Vaulkhurst fascinated her. It was a challenge to give the literary world the truth about his life—a truth as yet unpublished which might shed some light on his enigmatic writings. It was far more important to her than she could adequately explain to her mother and father at that point. If she succeeded it would be an achievement that would make her a more worthy individual in their eyes and give her one bright accomplishment to score beside the many successes of her brilliant brother and sister. She certainly understood enough about human emotions to see the hunger for acceptance and approbation from her family behind her desires. But it was more than that—a desperate need for the grown woman in her to make herself known, to face her own needs and desires as an adult.

Her mother was still frowning and attempting to adjust to this side of her daughter she had not seen before. She repeated, "I really think this should be given some more thought. . . ."

"Will you fly down?" Deborah's mother asked.

Two days had passed. Deborah's summer plans had at last become a *fait accompli* with her family. Her mother had reluctantly become resigned and was helping her pack. With Dr. Margaret Denhoff's usual helplessness in the face of anything practical, her assistance resulted mainly in her getting in the way while Deborah attempted to pack her suitcase.

"No," Deborah replied to her question. "I'm going to drive down there."

Her mother looked as if she were suddenly distrustful of her hearing aid. "But, Deborah, you can't drive."

"Well," Deborah admitted, refolding some undergarments her mother had packed for her, "I suppose the time has come to confess, Mother. I've been taking driving lessons the past couple of months. It got to be pretty embarrassing—a woman my age not being able to drive a car."

"But you were always too nervous to drive."

"Yes—I think I'm finally getting over some of my silly phobias. Once I got into the driving course, it was really fun. The instructor told me I did quite well."

"I'm amazed. I'm—I'm very pleased, Deborah. I think that's quite an accomplishment." Dr. Denhoff was looking at her daughter in a curious way, as if not quite certain what to make of her offspring. For Deborah had led a sheltered campus life, totally under the domination of her family, so that this change in her was more than a little disconcerting. The fledgling was about to venture out of the nest. Some fledgling, Deborah thought—twenty-four years old!

She glanced up to see her pixielike face reflected in the bedroom mirror. She took a serious, objective look at herself. She wasn't all that hard to look at, she thought. She'd never thought of herself as a raving beauty, certainly. She had a small, well-shaped nose and dark, close-cropped hair, which was neat and stylish. It contrasted with her large green eyes framed with long eyelashes—probably her best feature—and gave her an unusual coloring combination that some people said was striking. *Pert,* she thought, was a more appropriate adjective to describe her. Pert girls often had spunk, a quality she envied and one she lacked. But this new adventure was designed to teach her how to rely on herself, and maybe she'd find out if she had any spunk concealed under her compliant exterior. Just because she was petite, delicate-looking, and soft didn't mean there was no core of strength buried somewhere inside her.

"I'm going to buy a little car for the trip," she told her mother. Might as well drop all the bombshells at once. "It's a small, white, European-made sports car. I already have it picked out, and I love it. There's that small inheritance from Grandfather Denhoff, you know. I plan to use it to buy the car and to live on during the summer."

Deborah felt guilty at suddenly unloading so much startling information on her mother, who was making a valiant effort to adjust to her daughter's metamorphosis.

"I do hope you'll be careful," Dr. Denhoff said. "That's a long trip, and highway travel is so dangerous these days—" .

"There! All done." Deborah closed the latch on her suitcase. She drew a deep breath and sat on the side of her bed. She felt a bit lightheaded—slightly intoxicated, perhaps—from all the daring moves she was making in her new role as adventuress and traveler. At the moment she was in a state of euphoria. She wouldn't permit herself to think how she would feel when the temporary high wore off. Instead, she thought, she must plunge right ahead, keeping totally absorbed in her research project. "Mother, could you give me any leads on how I should proceed in this business of Cousin Clement's biographical material once I get to Uromund?"

Dr. Denhoff took a seat on the vanity bench, giving the question some thought before replying. "Well, you're not going to get much help from Clement. He'll probably be furious when he learns what you're doing there. I heard he once sicced his dogs on a television crew who went down there to interview him. You might try to talk with Aunt Christina Fallon, his foster mother. She could tell you a lot about him. Incidentally, she used to have a box full of Clement's early writings—diaries and journals that would be most useful—but she guards them jealously. Several universities, including this one, have made attempts to acquire them from her, but she won't even discuss the matter. I'd better write letters of introduction for you, but I warn you, she's an eccentric old recluse. I have no idea what kind of reception she'll give you."

"I think you said she's your great-aunt?"

"Yes . . . and your great-great-aunt. That makes Clement your cousin several times removed, though of course there's no actual blood relation since he was adopted."

"Aunt Christina lives in Uromund, too?"

"Oh, yes. At least she did the last we heard, and I'm

sure she wouldn't leave. She's lived in the same house all her life. Anyone in Uromund call tell you where it is."

They fell silent for a moment. Then Deborah said, "Y'know, it wasn't until this past year, while taking courses in contemporary American literature, that I became fascinated by Clement Vaulkhurst. I felt quite a thrill to think that he's really in our family, even if very distantly. You knew Cousin Clement quite well, Mother. Tell me what you know about him. What kind of man is he, really?"

Her mother smoothed a strand of her gray hair into place, gave the question some thought, then said, "Clement is a complex person, difficult to describe. Let's see . . . he would be in his late thirties now. As a boy he was an inventive, imaginative child, and quite adventurous. It was he who thought up the games he played with his friends—most original games. He was Clement Fallon then, his adopted name. But he had that legally changed back to his original family name, Vaulkhurst, when he began to write. As a young man in college, he was intense, with his own way of thinking and doing things, which made him something of a misfit on campus. He has a streak of arrogance and insolence that some people admire and others dislike. As you young people put it, he wanted to 'do his own thing.' After college, he went back to Uromund to publish a little weekly newspaper. No one in the family could understand why a man of his brilliant nature would be content with such a modest career. But it supplied his material needs—mainly books—and gave him time for his writing and studies. And Clement Vaulkhurst was never a man to give a hang what other people thought of him."

Deborah felt a peculiar shiver run up her spine. From some of the things she'd heard about Clement Vaulkhurst—his arrogance, his ego, his ruthlessness with women—she had intensely disliked him personally. And yet she found herself envious of the qualities her mother had just described. How she wished she had that kind of courage—to do her own thing and not give a hang about what the rest of the world thought! Perhaps it was that fascination with his character that was drawing her to Uromund to delve into the life of this intriguing man.

"So many critics compare him to William Blake," she said.

Her mother nodded. "Yes. Of all the world's great poets and writers, Blake held a particular fascination for Clement. It was because of his mysticism, I think. Clement claimed to be the only man who ever lived who fully understood the underlying philosophical meaning in Blake's myths." She hesitated, then, with some embarrassment, added, "Clement said he often communicated with Blake."

"D'you suppose," Deborah asked with a giggle, "that Cousin Clement had, as the English say, 'gone round the bend'?"

"No. There's nothing wrong with Clement's mind. He always had a flair for the theatrical. He likes to shock people, make them uncomfortable. If you ask me, Clement was secretly laughing at stuffy literary critics. He liked to play a monstrous joke on life and people."

"Do you think he's working on a new novel? If I could preview an unpublished Clement Vaulkhurst manuscript, I would drop something of a bombshell in literary circles."

"Yes, but I wouldn't count on anything like that. More than likely, Clement will not allow you to get within throwing distance of anything he's working on. He may even sic his dogs on you!"

Spring semester ended and the Denhoff family departed from the campus. Deborah's father was off to explore Mayan ruins in Central America, and her mother was going to a symposium in New York. Deborah packed her bags into her brand-new sports car. She was seen off by a forlorn Bill Hughbank. "I'll be in touch," he promised. "If you decide to chuck this whole business, give me a call and I'll fly down."

"Yes, Bill," she said.

"I may fly down anyway."

"Well . . ." She tried to think of a way to discourage that without hurting his feelings too badly. She really wanted this summer to herself.

He took advantage of her hesitation to lean over the car door for a goodbye kiss. A wave of fondness for him—or was it guilt?—made her return the kiss with more warmth than he expected. That brightened him but only made Deborah feel more guilty. She really needed to make up her mind about Bill before she went on encouraging him. She might want to break the engagement completely before the summer ended.

But as she put the car in gear and started down the tree-shaded street that wound out of the campus, other thoughts pushed Bill Hughbank out of her mind. She took a farewell glance back at the rambling old Cape Cod home where she'd spent most of her life. Her palms were suddenly cold and sweaty. She gritted her teeth, fighting off a wave of panic. She forced her eyes away from her home. She was not going to give in to the old feelings, she told herself sternly. This was the start of a great adventure. Nevertheless, she could not shake off a premonition that her life was never going to be the same again after today. And she wasn't sure yet if she was going to like what lay ahead of her.

Chapter Two

Deborah's trip to Uromund was uneventful. She drove at moderate speeds, becoming familiar with her new car, absorbing the scenery and eating her picnic lunches in roadside parks. With each passing day as she successfully negotiated the highway traffic, coping with her newly found independence, her self-confidence strengthened.

By noon of the sixth day, she had crossed the state line into Texas and was on a highway that cut a slash between great walls of towering pine forests near the Louisiana border. She was entering the area known as the Big Thicket.

Before leaving home, she had studied the background of this area extensively, for its primitive wilderness and areas of isolation had undoubtedly contributed to the brooding, contemplative mood in Vaulkhurst's novels.

The junglelike growth that sprawled over swamps and rivers contained a stunning array of botanical and zoological specimens. In some of the virgin areas, where the chain saws of lumber companies had not ravaged the natural beauty, there were more than two hundred varieties of trees and shrubs. Some forty species of wild orchids bloomed in the jungle habitat. There were thirty varieties of ferns, and four of the continent's five species of carnivorous plants existed here.

Roaming the woods were still to be found bear, deer, the rare Texas red wolf, and a nearly extinct species of panther. Alligators slithered across the murky waters of the swamps, and snakes of all sizes and descriptions were abundant.

The birds that made their home here were of particular interest to Deborah, since bird watching was one of her hobbies. She had brought along her binoculars in hopes of sighting one of the huge black, white, and red woodpeckers that were said to grow larger than chicken hawks. Among the three hundred kinds of birds here were reportedly such rare varieties as the Backman warbler, the roseate spoonbill, and America's only stork, the wood ibis, as well as the golden eagle.

Once, Deborah had read, this botanical garden of nature had covered three million acres, unspoiled by human civilization. Now it was slashed by highways, scarred by sawmills, oil fields, ranches, and small towns, and defaced by paper and wood companies. There were still some three hundred thousand acres of the Big Thicket proper. In the area were great man-made lakes and national forests. Uromund was off the beaten path, an isolated community far back on the fringe of the dense swampland.

At midafternoon, following the direction of her road map, she turned onto a narrow farm-to-market road that dissolved into the forest. The road, though hard-topped, was in poor repair. She drove slowly in the perpetual twilight of the ancient woods. Around her towered longleaf pines, sweetbay magnolias, and giant cypress. Some of them must have been saplings when the Declaration of Independence was signed. She had driven for miles in this hushed world without seeing a living soul when at last she came upon a sign on the shoulder of the road that read Uromund—City Limits.

A town of some five thousand inhabitants seemed oddly misplaced in this dead-end isolation. But she had read that it had survived because of lumbering companies that operated in this area. The old town dated to pre–Civil War days when wealthy Louisiana plantation owners, making their fortunes in lumber and turpentine, built mansions along the river near the town. Deborah's mother had told her that Clement Vaulkhurst had restored one of those antebellum Southern mansions and had made it his home.

Weariness from the trip was forgotten as she slowly cruised through the town. With a thrill of excitement, she thought that the famous novelist had walked on these very streets, gone into the post office, sat on the bench in the courthouse square. Anyone who had ever read a Vaulkhurst novel would recognize the town at once. This was the village of Osweega, the setting for all his mythical novels. He had described it in meticulous detail—a fact which had no doubt caused much uneasiness among the local citizenry and was probably the cause for bitterness toward him by some of them.

The heart of the village, as in so many small

Southern towns, was the courthouse square. On its lawn was a rusty cannon and a Civil War monument. The courthouse was a huge, gloomy building of weathered sandstone huddled under the shade from great oak trees. The business buildings around the town square appeared to have been constructed at the turn of the century. The streets were narrow, designed to accommodate horses and buggies rather than automobiles.

She saw hardly a soul on the streets, though it was too early for the stores to have closed. Suddenly, she had the irrational feeling that this town did not actually exist. It was a page from a Vaulkhurst novel. She had become nothing more than a story character, a literary invention of the author with no soul or will of her own, moving through the novelist's dream world. She shuddered at her overactive imagination.

She stopped at a filling station for directions to a motel and was advised that the town's one motel was located on the northern outskirts. She drove there expecting the worst, but was pleased to find a cluster of a dozen clean, modern red-brick cabins attractively nestled among the pine trees. A sign read PINEVIEW LODGES.

She drove around to the office, parked her car on the graveled drive, and entered through a screen door. The place was deserted. She rang a bell on the counter and called several times but got no reply.

She walked outside and looked around, at a loss to know what to do next. Then she spied a figure coming from a shed some distance behind the cabins. As he drew nearer, she saw he was a deeply tanned man in his early thirties, dressed casually in blue jeans and a T-shirt. He was carrying some fishing rods which he put into the bed of a pickup truck before ambling over to where Deborah stood. "Hello," he said, giving her a disarming smile.

She assumed he was somehow employed here. "Are there any vacancies?" she asked, somewhat shortly.

He smiled again. "Reckon so," he drawled.

It was difficult to remain exasperated at such a friendly smile. "Well, which cabin is available?" she asked, softening her tone a bit.

He looked around at the buildings, rubbing his jaw. Then his cheerful blue eyes returned to her. "To tell the truth, ma'am, I guess they all are."

"Really? But you have the only motel in town."

"Yes. Not many people stop off here. Last week I had a gentleman from the East on a business trip for one of the lumber companies. Very nice fellow. Played dominoes with me in the evenings—"

"Well, I'd like to get unpacked. Which cabin would you recommend?"

"Well, they're all exactly alike."

"How about that one?" She picked one at random.

"Fine. Want me to help you with your bags?"

"That would be nice."

He went to the office, got a key, and led the way to the unit Deborah had picked out. When she stepped inside, she was again pleasantly surprised. It was entirely modern, air-conditioned, it even boasted a color television set. It was as attractive as anything she'd seen on her trip, and it was spotlessly clean.

"This is very nice. It will do just fine."

"Good," he said with his ready smile. "How long will you be staying?"

"I'm not sure. You see, I plan to spend the entire summer in Uromund, but I won't be able to afford a motel room that long. I'll have to look for a rooming house."

"We could make special rates," he suggested.

"Well—I'll talk to you about that after I'm more settled and have a chance to look around. Should I sign the register now?"

He shrugged. "You can do that any time. I'm on my way to go fishing now."

"Won't there be someone in the office?"

"Nope."

She stared at him. Then he said, "Oh, my name's Doug Carpenter. I'm the owner—day and night clerk, too."

"How do you do. I'm Deborah Denhoff. If you don't mind my saying so, Mr. Carpenter, you have a rather casual way of running your business."

"Well, like I say, not many people stay here, and I'd rather go fishing anyway. Why did you come to Uromund?" he suddenly asked.

She hesitated before answering. It was really none of his business. But then, in a town this size, everyone would soon know her business anyway. And perhaps he could help. He certainly seemed friendly and obliging. So she explained briefly how she had come to spend the summer researching the life of Clement Vaulkhurst.

She didn't know what sort of reaction she had expected, but she certainly had expected *something*. Instead, he just looked at her in his patient, smiling fashion, his face totally bland and inscrutable.

"You—you know who Clement Vaulkhurst is, I assume?"

"Sure. Best tourist attraction this town has—that big house where he lives. He's kind of a weirdo."

"He *is* the most brilliant American writer of modern

times," she said rather sharply, surprised at her sudden loyalty to a man she had never met. "He was awarded both the Nobel and Pulitzer prizes."

"I know. I rent cabins to people who come down to gawk at that big mansion where he lives and see the town he wrote about. But he's still pretty strange."

Deborah smiled in spite of herself. She could imagine how a provincial little isolated backwoods town would react to a genius like Clement Vaulkhurst in its midst. In a community like this, people operated hardware stores or filling stations. They did not write great books.

"Do you by any chance know a Christina Fallon? She's my aunt."

"Miss Christina? Sure. Everybody in the county knows her. Now, *she's* weird!"

"Seems to be a lot of that going around," she said, feeling irritated at him again. "Could you tell me how I could get to Clement Vaulkhurst's home from here?"

Deborah arrived at the Clement Vaulkhurst mansion after driving several miles beyond Uromund on a little-traveled dirt road. The house was indeed isolated, hidden by a heavy growth of trees and brush. It was surrounded by a swampy area that reminded Deborah of an ancient moat protecting a castle. The mansion itself was on higher ground, its stately white columns giving it an air of haughty pride in the rays of the late-afternoon sun.

The grounds, which covered several acres, were surrounded by a formidable high fence. It required all of her strength to drag open a ponderous gate. She drove into the grounds, closed the gate, and then,

remembering her mother's warning that Clement had a
pack of mean dogs, hastily got back into the car and
proceeded up the graveled drive.

The vast lawn was freshly mowed and the hedges
were neatly trimmed. The attention the grounds re-
ceived indicated that Clement kept a capable and
industrious caretaker.

The house itself was an anomaly in this provincial
backwoods area. It looked as if it had been bodily
picked up from Beverly Hills and placed here—or,
more appropriately, as if it had materialized out of an
antebellum plantation. It was built in the style of
Louisiana Creole classic architecture, a mixture of
Greek revivial and Georgian influences. Ionic columns
lent an air of stately dignity to the front veranda.

Above the entrance, Vaulkhurst had placed, in
carved oak letters, an inscription by Virgil, *Felix qui
potuit rerum cognoscere causas.* "Happy he who has
been able to know the reasons for things."

Was Clement Vaulkhurst referring to himself? Probably, she thought. Apparently, the man's conceit knew
no bounds. He was insufferable. Yet, she had to admit,
he was also fascinating. According to the rumors about
him, numerous women had found him fatally attractive.

Deborah parked her car and walked up to the front
door. She rapped the massive knocker several times.
The sound reverberated inside the house, but there was
no reply and no other sound inside. The house appeared to be deserted. She kept a wary eye out for
dogs, prepared to beat a hasty retreat to her car if
necessary.

She drew a deep breath and called "Hello!" loudly,

several times. Like the sound of the door knocker, her voice echoed around the building, but no one answered.

She stood on the threshold, undecided about her next move. Then she heard dogs barking off behind the building somewhere. She went back to her car and sat behind the wheel.

A wave of disappointment swept over her. She had been driving since early morning. She was keyed up with the prospect of coming face to face with her illustrious and intriguing relative. Anticipation had imbued her with a courage and sense of initiative she usually felt lacking. It took a certain amount of nerve to go boldly knocking on Clement Vaulkhurst's front door after the dire warnings her mother had given her about the novelist. She might lose that nerve if she went back to the motel, slept off the keen edge of her tense enthusiasm, and returned in the cold light of morning.

On a sudden inspiration, she started the engine of her car and followed the drive that circled the mansion. It led back under a grove of trees to a neat brick cottage, which she assumed was the abode of the caretaker. Here she caught sight of the pack of dogs that were barking so ferociously. They were in a dog run behind the brick cottage, kept imprisoned by a heavy chain-link fence.

She parked her car in front of the caretaker's house, made a face at the dogs, and walked up to the door. She was about to knock when she spied a note pinned to the doorframe: *Andrew, I have gone into Houston for the day. Will be back sometime late this afternoon. Clement.*

Obviously, the caretaker was off somewhere, for he

had not gotten the note. Did that mean she was alone on the premises? Or had Clement returned and simply was not answering the front door?

Since no one had come out to run her off, she decided to make use of this opportunity to make notes and take pictures of the Vaulkhurst mansion, something she might not be permitted to do after Clement put in an appearance.

She drove back around to the front of the big house. There, she got her 35-mm. camera out of its case and slowly strolled around the luxurious home, taking pictures from several angles.

She had walked almost completely around the building when her roving gaze spied a back door ajar. She frowned thoughtfully. "Cousin Clement, are you in there?" she wondered aloud. After what her mother had said about Clement, it was entirely possible that he had returned from Houston and had been in the house all along but refused to answer the door.

She gathered up her courage, thrust her head through the open door, and called, "Clement Vaulkhurst? This is Deborah Denhoff. I am a relative of yours. I'm down here on a visit. May I come in?"

No reply. But she heard someone stirring around inside the house.

"Hello!" she persisted.

Still no reply.

"I've driven all the way down from Connecticut. Please let me come in," she begged.

The new *her,* the awakening, independent adult deep inside, clamoring to be recognized, urged her not to give up. She swallowed hard, steeled her resolve, and stepped inside the doorway. She was surprised at her own stubbornness. But *somebody* was in the house, and she was going to persist until she evoked a response. The worst that could happen, she thought, was that she would be tossed out.

She found herself in a hallway. It led her to the front of the house, to a large entrance foyer that had a marble floor. Here a winding stairway led to the second floor. Turning to her left, she saw an open doorway to a book-lined study. Was this where the illustrious author worked? Her pulse began racing furiously. Again she called his name as she stepped timidly to the study doorway.

Then she saw the source of living sounds inside the house. A huge black tomcat gave her a suspicious glare and jumped down from a desk. The tension melted from her body, leaving her weak. She laughed shakily. "You old rascal! You sure had me fooled."

She moved through the doorway into the study, and the portrait of Clement Vaulkhurst that hung on the wall of the study virtually leaped out at her. She was not prepared for the effect the startling likeness had on her.

Vaulkhurst detested having his picture taken, so few photographs of him existed. Deborah had had only a vague idea what he looked like. But now she stood before his portrait, transfixed, immobilized by luminous eyes that were black as chips of coal. They burned into the depths of her being with relentless fury. They were the eyes of a man who had known torment in a restless pursuit of the heights and depths of human experience. She remembered that her mother had said that Clement Vaulkhurst claimed to have made a pact with the devil. She could almost believe it, for her distant cousin's portrait shimmered with black rays of satanic power. His eyes smoldered with defiance and scorn. He had a rough, dark complexion, jet-black hair with a touch of gray at the temples, and hard, chiseled features with lines like deep knife slashes around the mouth and eyes. His diabolically sardonic grin both repulsed and fascinated her. It was the face of a man in control of his own destiny who didn't care what the rest of the world thought of him, a man who made and lived by his own rules. His mouth was at the same time ruthless, arrogant, and sensual. Yet it was only there, around the mouth, that she also detected the shadow of something else—the sensitivity of a creative artist.

She had no idea how long she stood there under the hypnotic spell of that remarkable portrait. When at last she looked away, she shivered.

Slowly, she moved about the room. Everywhere she looked, everything she touched, seemed to vibrate with the power of the man. She could feel his presence as surely as if he were standing a few feet behind her. It was an awesome experience, both frightening and inspiring. She felt flushed and pressed her palms against her warm cheeks. She'd never had anything affect her quite like this before.

Her gaze was attracted to one of the books on the desk, a leather-bound collection of poems by William Blake. She thought about the strong literary ties between Vaulkhurst and the eighteenth-century English writer. She was reading aloud some of the curious, haunting lines of the long-dead poet when something caused her to look up. What it was she could not be sure—a faint rustling sound, a movement in the hushed room, a subtle change in temperature? It had been one or all or perhaps none of those things that had attracted her attention. But she had felt that sensation one has when another being enters the room.

"Must be the cat again," she chuckled, her voice not entirely steady. But the big old tomcat had run out when she walked into the room and was nowhere to be seen.

The self-conscious feeling of being an intruder grew until it overwhelmed her. She was insane to be here, she realized. There was no telling what Clement Vaulkhurst would do if he caught her in his house. He might even have her put in jail for illegal entry! What had possessed her to come wandering into the man's innermost sanctum?

The inexplicable mood of boldness that had thrust her into this situation suddenly deserted her. It was replaced by a panicky need to escape. She hurried back down the hallway and through the back door she had found ajar. Not until she was outside, breathing the cool dusk air, did she feel at ease again.

She'd really had no business poking around his home like that. But she had fallen under a strange kind of enchantment that she could not explain. She returned to her car and settled into the comfortable bucket seat, suddenly aware of how weary she was from the long drive down here.

She leaned back against the headrest. When she closed her eyes, the fierce countenance of Clement Vaulkhurst blazed across the screen of her imagination. A languid sensation stole over her. She had never before in her life felt in such a poignant mood. She felt strangely sad, as if she might cry, yet alive with a curious sense of anticipation. A warmth began stealing through her body, making her nerve ends tingle. Soon she fell into a languorous sleep, and Clement Vaulkhurst was at the center of her dream. She imagined what his voice would be like, how the touch of his hand would feel. She imagined they were having a candle-light dinner. In the shadows, he leaned closer. His voice had a deep, resonant quality that charmed her senses. . . .

Then, like a dash of icy water, something brought her awake. It was a man's hand, grasping her shoulder and shaking her.

She heard his angry baritone voice. "Young woman, what are you doing trespassing on my property?"

And she looked up not at a portrait but at the scowling countenance of a very real, alive Clement Vaulkhurst, angry enough to breathe fire!

"Oh!" Deborah gasped, momentarily stunned by shock and surprise.

"I asked what you are doing on my property," he growled, his large fingers biting into the soft flesh of her shoulder.

"Please," she whimpered. "You're hurting my shoulder. If you'll let go, I can explain."

The black eyes burned intensely in the stern face of Clement Vaulkhurst. Without softening his scowl, he slowly released his powerful grip from her shoulder. She rubbed the stinging area with her other hand and wondered why she felt like a child caught with her hand in the cookie jar. She hadn't committed any crime, so why did she feel so guilty? It was that same old feeling her parents had always stirred up in her before she had found the courage to assert herself. Realizing that he had brought that hated feeling back, she became angry and met his scowl with blazing eyes.

"Well?" he demanded. "I'm waiting for your expla-nation."

Deborah fought down that old subservient feeling she was hoping to forever extinguish from her repertoire of emotions and held on to her anger. "I'm a relative of yours," she said haughtily, raising her chin defiantly.

His scowl deepened as he glared at her more closely in the darkness. "A relative? What kind of relative?"

"I'm your cousin—sort of. Second or third, I guess," she admitted. "I can't exactly figure it out, to be honest."

"Young woman," he said impatiently, "you aren't making much sense."

"You wouldn't, either, if you'd just had the wits frightened out of you. Don't you know you could give a person a heart attack, sneaking up on them like that?"

"I wasn't 'sneaking up' on you," he said, his voice dripping acid. "I was attempting to find out why you found it necessary to park your car in my private driveway in order to take a nap."

"I fell asleep because I have been driving since early this morning and I'm exhausted. I was waiting for you to come back so I could talk to you, and I guess I fell asleep."

He made an impatient gesture with his hand. "Please spare me the boring details of your driving and sleeping habits. Why did you want to see me, and what's this rubbish about being my second or third cousin?"

His supercilious attitude added fuel to her anger. His entire manner implied that she was some kind of retarded child. "My mother is Margaret Denhoff," she said in words chiseled from ice. "Does that mean anything to you?"

"It might," he said suspiciously. "If you are telling the truth."

She fumbled in her purse. "I have a letter of

introduction from my mother. Would you care to read it?" She thrust it at him.

He looked as if he were trying to decide whether to accept the letter or unleash his dogs on her. Finally he growled. "Oh, very well. Come on into the house. I can't very well read your blasted letter out here in the dark." He stalked off toward the front door of the mansion.

Deborah got her car door open and ran after him, wondering if the head of the English department would let her change the subject of her thesis.

Vaulkhurst opened the door, then turned and scowled at her again. "This had better be valid. I've had newspaper people try various underhand tricks to get an interview out of me."

She was too tired and too angry to reply. She followed him sullenly into the house.

He switched on the lights and went directly to the study. For the first time she saw him clearly, the living counterpart of the striking portrait that had had such an emotional effect on her. Her cheeks were suddenly aflame as she thought about the thoughts the portrait had stirred in her and the dream she'd had about him. Confused emotions stormed through her. She was humiliated, wondering if he could see her feelings in her face. In the five minutes she had known him in person, she had learned to despise him. His arrogance, conceit, and rudeness infuriated her. Any adolescent fantasies she might have had about him had turned to ashes. Now she couldn't imagine feeling romantic about him if he were the last man on earth!

He sat at his desk and quickly read the note from her mother. Then he took a bottle of brandy from a cabinet, poured a dollop in each of two snifters, and placed them on the desk. He sat on the edge of the desk, giving her a thorough scrutiny.

"So you're Margaret's girl," he said, in a somewhat more civil voice. "Yes, of course I know your mother. I was always quite fond of her, as a matter of fact. She visited here in Uromund several times when I was growing up. She brought you along once, as I recall. You were a rather ugly, scrawny thing then, about six years old. Do you remember?"

"No, I don't," she said, her voice still cold.

His gaze continued a bold inventory of her face and figure.

"Well," he remarked at last, having completed his scrutiny, "I must say you grew out of the ugly-duckling stage rather nicely. If you got rid of those frumpy clothes and dowdy flat shoes and learned how to use makeup, you might even be attractive."

Her anger, which had dropped to a low, steady beat, suddenly became a crescendo. "I don't recall that I asked for any advice from you about my appearance!"

He chuckled. "So you do have a bit of spunk hidden under that meek, English-country girl exterior. Very nice. Lights up your eyes. Incidentally, your large green eyes are one of your best features. You should play them up."

She spluttered with rage. "You're insufferable."

"So I've been told," he agreed with a maddening smile. "However, I've also been told I have remarkable taste in women. Since we're relatives—'kissing cousins,' I think, is that awful, trite Southern term—I thought I'd give you a bit of friendly advice. Actually, the difference in our age makes me feel a bit more like an uncle."

And you're doing your best to make me feel like that scrawny, freckle-faced six-year-old child you described, she thought furiously.

Then he seemed to remember the brandy he had poured. He picked up one of the snifters and handed her the other.

"No, thank you," she said coldly.

"Good heavens, don't tell me you're a teetotaler, too, to go along with those square clothes."

"Of course not!" she snapped. She took the glass and gulped the amber liquid, gasping as it burned its way down her throat.

"For heaven's sake, child," he admonished, "that's fifty-year-old brandy you just insulted. You're supposed to savor it, not swill it!"

"I know how to drink brandy," she choked after she got over her coughing spell. "It's just that you've made me so furious I don't know what I'm doing. Why are you insulting me this way? Why are you being so unpleasant? Why are you trying your best to make me feel like some kind of dowdy provincial from hicksville?"

He studied her with one raised eyebrow, gently rocking the brandy glass under his nostrils as he savored the bouquet of the fine liquor. "Just trying to become acquainted, my dear. I don't have the time or patience for the polite façade the average person presents in polite company. It's artificial and false." He enjoyed a sip of the brandy, put the glass on the desk, then rubbed his hands together and said, "Now, then. Do you want to tell me what you're doing here? Surely you didn't drive three thousand miles to get my autograph. You didn't come here to borrow money, did you? Or did you? If you did, the answer is no."

"Certainly not!" she retorted. "I wouldn't cross the street to get your autograph!"

He threw his head back and laughed uproariously.

Before encountering him face to face, she would have given a different answer. For the past year she had worshiped at the shrine of his literary genius. She would have treasured signed copies of his novels. But he had so infuriated her that now she planned to burn all of the books of his that she owned at the first opportunity.

When he had finished laughing, he said, "Well? You haven't answered my question."

She hesitated. Then she held out her empty brandy glass. "First, could I have another drink, please?"

"Certainly. If this time you promise to be a bit more civil to a highly civilized liquor."

"Now," he said after he had poured her drink, "you were going to tell me why you drove all the way down here to see me."

She waited to reply until she drank the brandy, taking care to sip it in appropriate fashion this time, then being angry with herself that she hadn't defiantly tossed it down. At the moment she felt like telling him that she had just dropped by on her way through town and then forever shaking the dust of this place from her feet. On the other hand, the anger he had stirred in her, plus two brandys on an empty stomach, gave her all the courage she needed to tell him she wanted to interview him for her thesis.

She came to the sudden resolve that she was going to do the thesis, and if he gave her any trouble about it, so much the better. She was going to succeed in prying under the surface of his hard, cynical exterior where other journalistic and literary investigators had failed. She had come down here with idealistic zeal. It had been replaced with a fury to hit him where it hurt him the most—to penetrate and expose his precious privacy!

"I'm working on my master's degree in English," she said. "This summer I am writing my thesis. I plan to write the thesis on the personal side of Clement Vaulkhurst."

In the deathly silence that followed, some of her angry resolve faltered. She felt her hand which held the empty brandy glass tremble slightly.

He was staring at her as if wondering about the validity of his hearing. "A thesis. About me," he said slowly. "A dreary, dull, inept college thesis. About *me*." Where before he had treated her with a kind of fond, amused contempt, he suddenly became coldly angry. "My dear young woman . . . James Boswell, a literary giant, wrote the life of Samuel Johnson. If and when I ever accept a biographer, it will be a literary master on the level of James Boswell. Not a mousy graduate student from a dinky one-horse college scribbling a ridiculous *thesis!*"

White-lipped with fury, Deborah faced the novelist like a dueling adversary about to draw pistols at dawn. "I came here to get this material," she said evenly. "My college degree depends on it. And I plan to do so, with or without your help."

"Well, you'll certainly do so without my help—and perhaps against my active opposition. I might even sue you."

She drew herself up to her full height. "Freel fee to do so!" she said haughtily. Then, realizing that her tongue was playing tricks on her, she stammered, "I mean, you don't inminidate—intinderdate—I mean . . ."

He was staring at her, his anger dissolving into infuriating amusement. "You're getting pie-eyed! When did you eat last?"

She waved her hand. "Hamburger—noon . . ."

He grinned, flashing white teeth against his dark complexion. "Two glasses of fifty-year-old brandy on an empty stomach. You're stoned all right, little graduate student."

"I can hold my liquor jus' fine, thank you," she said with haughty dignity. "Now, I think I'll be going."

She would die before admitting that her head was swimming furiously. The brandy had hit her with sudden and devastating force. She turned to the door, making a valiant effort to keep a steady course.

He came around from the desk and took her arm. "You can't drive. I won't permit it."

"What 'd'ya mean, you won't permit it? You're not my father!"

"No. But he isn't here, and I'm responsible. You are under my roof and I served you the alcohol, not realizing that you're not grown up enough for hard liquor."

"How dare you say that!" she said, furiously trying to disentangle her arm. "I'm perfectly capa—capabuble of drivin' a car." She stumbled, and he caught her.

"That does it," he said firmly. "You're spending the night in the guest room. In the morning, when you're sober, you are welcome to drive away. In fact, I would encourage it, and I would advise you not to stop until you are back in your home state. Tonight, however, you will stay here. I won't have it on my conscience that you killed yourself because of my brandy."

"What conscience?" she demanded. "Take your hands off me!"

For an answer, he picked her up easily and tossed her over his shoulder like a sack of grain. Furiously, she beat on his powerful back with her clenched fists, but he merely laughed at her. He carried her up the spiral stairway and deposited her on the carpet in front of a bedroom door.

"Now," he said, "I want you to get a good night's sleep. And here's something to think about when you're drifting off. This is what you should be doing instead of writing a ridiculous thesis for which you probably have no talent whatsoever. . . ."

His powerful arms swept her up against him and his mouth crushed down on hers.

She was caught totally by surprise, too shocked to resist. Foggily, she remembered the portrait over the mantelpiece. She struggled against him, determined, suddenly, to wrench herself away from his smothering embrace. But his powerful arms held her to him even tighter. She felt his strong chest muscles press warmly against the swell of her breasts. An unexpected tingle shot through her, heating the depths of her being in a way that was both pleasurable and agonizing. Something she couldn't define, something she had never felt before, stirred in her . . . some kind of primitive longing, a nebulous hunger that grew in her as she felt her anger dissolve. It was the alcohol, she assured herself, that was making her feel so abandoned and careless. It was as if she were floating in some never-never land where time and space melted together and today was just a glimmer of what a few minutes before had been reality. Her thoughts swam as his lips drained all resistance from her. Suddenly, she found herself pressing her breasts against the wall of his chest, her arms thrown around his neck, pulling him down to her, drinking in the delicious nectar of his mouth.

A faint aroma of pipe tobacco and shaving lotion assailed her nostrils, emphasizing the masculinity of this man who was setting her on fire with his touch. A throbbing began to jolt her body. A desire for fulfillment raced through her. In that instant, she became oblivious to thoughts about convention and social inhibitions. Her emotions and her body cried out for more of this man, for more of his touch, for more of his kisses. . . .

Then he released her and stepped back. She saw his taunting smile, his dark, scornful eyes. "Good night, 'kissing cousin.' Pleasant dreams." And he turned and strode away.

Chapter Three

Deborah awoke with a start. She stared at the ceiling, totally disorganized. Where was she? She sat up and then gasped as she became aware of a pounding headache.

She pressed her fingertips against her throbbing temples and looked around the room, frowning. Then the memory of last night's humiliating experience came back with a rush. Her face flamed.

"The nerve of that man!" she exclaimed, remembering how he had casually tossed her over his shoulder, carried her upstairs, and then kissed her shamelessly.

Well, she thought, I'm not getting off to a very good start with the subject of my thesis. Already he thinks I'm some kind of naïve schoolgirl, and I think he's a beast!

She tried to stand up. The room swam. She clutched a bedpost until her equilibrium became more reliable. Then she walked unsteadily to a dresser. She winced when she saw her image. She had fallen across the bed last night and slept in her clothes, which were of course now totally disheveled. Her hair was tangled. "You're a mess," she told her image.

She found an adjoining bathroom, where she splashed cold water in her face and made what repairs she could.

Then she drew a deep breath, squared her shoulders, and opened her bedroom door. She dreaded coming face to face with Clement Vaulkhurst this morning. With some luck, she hoped, she could quietly slip out of the house, get in her car, and drive back to the motel without confronting her host.

The big old house seemed quiet and deserted. She hoped Clement had gone somewhere. She made it to the foot of the stairs, and then a masculine voice said, "Miss Denhoff?"

Startled, she spun around and instantly regretted the sudden movement, which jolted the devils in her head into a renewed frenzy of pounding. "Y-yes . . .?"

The man who moved toward her from a room down the hallway was not Clement Vaulkhurst. "Good morning," he said. "I'm Andrew Smith, Mr. Vaulkhurst's gardener. He had to leave this morning, and he asked me to see after you when you woke up. Would you like some breakfast?"

He smiled in a disarming manner. His blue eyes were friendly. He was a middle-aged man whose brown hair was starting to turn gray at the temples. He was dressed in a brown work shirt and trousers.

"Th-thank you, Mr. Smith. I think I'll just drive on into town."

"You look a mite peaked, if you don't mind my saying so, ma'am. Mr. Vaulkhurst said you might be waking up with a hangover."

She felt her cheeks turn scarlet. "He did, did he? Well, I'm quite all right. I don't know why he told you a thing like that!" She raised her chin angrily and winced at the pain it stirred up.

He moved closer, still smiling. "I brew up a mighty tasty cup of hot tea. Nothing helps a person face a new day like a good, strong cup of tea."

Her pride weakened. "Well . . . I really would like a cup of tea . . ."

"Sure. Why don't you come on with me? Clement said we could use the kitchen here in the big house, but, to tell the truth, I'm more comfortable fussing around in my own place." He showed her the way out a back door and down the graveled path to the caretaker's cabin she had seen the day before. He opened the front door with a courteous gesture. There was an old-fashioned, courtly manner about him that put her at her ease and made her feel secure.

She found herself in a cozy, two-room bungalow. It was obviously a bachelor's quarters. There were deer-horn trophies on the walls. The furniture was Western style, practical and rugged. The place was scrupulously tidy.

A bookshelf held a predictable Zane Grey series. But there was also a Mark Twain collection and the complete works of Shakespeare and Dickens. She thought that her host had a broad range in reading tastes for a gardener. Curiously, there were no Vaulkhurst novels in the bookshelves, she noticed.

Soon the teapot whistled merrily while he fussed around with cups on the drainboard. The kitchen area was separated from the main living room by a counter-top pass-through bar. She took a seat on the bar stool.

Presently, he brought two steaming cups to the bar. She sipped the amber liquid eagerly. "Um . . . you brew a very tasty cup of tea, Mr. Smith."

He nodded. "I'm a tea drinker. Never did go much for coffee. Gives me heartburn." He had a sip of tea, then said, "So you're a relative of Clement's."

"Only a distant cousin. And no blood relation at that, since he was raised by an adopted mother, Aunt Christina, who is actually our relative. I'm a college student, working on my master's degree. I've decided to spend the summer down here, doing research on Clement Vaulkhurst for my thesis."

She suddenly wondered what this nice man must think of her. That darned Clement had told Andrew Smith she'd had too much to drink last night. Then she had spent the night unchaperoned in the home of Clement Vaulkhurst, a notorious seducer of women.

Her face reddened with embarrassment, and she lowered her gaze to her cup of tea. She felt his blue eyes regarding her speculatively. "I would imagine Clement would make pretty good subject material all right. Nobody has written the truth about him."

"Oh . . . Have you known him long?"

"Sure. I've known Clement off and on all my life. We went possum hunting together in the Thicket when we were schoolboys."

Deborah was instantly alert. "I'd like you to tell me about him. I need all the information I can get."

"Hmm." He pursed his lips thoughtfully. "That would take a bit of time. Sure you wouldn't like to have some breakfast?"

The hot tea had eased her headache, and now her stomach reminded her that she had not had a solid meal since noon the day before. "Thank you." She smiled. "I'm really ravenous."

"I was down to the creek early this morning, checking some trotlines I put out last night. Catfish bite at night," he explained. "Had a couple of nice blue channel cats on my line. Got 'em cleaned and all ready to fry. If you give me a few minutes, I'll fix you up a breakfast you'll remember a long time. If I say so myself, cooking is one of my better talents—one of the things I picked up knocking around the world."

She laughed. "I'm getting hungrier by the minute."

Deborah sat at the bar, sipping tea and chatting with him as he bustled about in his neat kitchen. Andrew Smith, she discovered, far from being a backwoods hick, was an interesting character who'd had quite a checkered career.

"Yes, Clement and I were pretty close friends as boys," he said. "We liked to hunt and explore the woods. Clement was much smarter than the average youngster. A lot of the things he talked about went over my head. But he liked being with me anyway because I knew those backwoods better than other kids. Clement liked doing things like collecting snakes and plants. It wasn't enough for him to just go off on a hike. He'd take along a botany book and look up the names of the trees and plants. He could look at any plant in the county and tell you what it was and what it was good for. A lot of things growing around here were medicine plants used by the Indians. Some were deadly poison. Clement knew all that stuff.

"But don't get the notion he was a sissy or a bookish kid. He could outrun and outfight and outlie any other kid in school. Especially outlie. I guess Clement was the greatest liar I ever ran across. He didn't make up little piddling lies. He made up the most outlandish, awesome fabrications you ever heard. Even as a kid, he had a wild imagination."

The cabin was filling with delicious aromas from the pan sizzling on the stove. Soon, Andrew placed before Deborah a plate heaped with chunks of golden-brown catfish and a plate of homemade biscuits.

He watched with a pleased grin as Deborah made sounds of ecstasy over the exquisite flavors. "This is simply delicious! I've never tasted homemade biscuits this light. And the fish—ummm!"

He chuckled, obviously proud of his culinary ability.

They were relaxed and comfortable. The atmosphere was friendly and homey. Andrew was clearly happy to have friendly companionship and someone to praise his cooking. He started talking about Clement Vaulkhurst again, and Deborah was all ears.

"When Clement and I reached high-school age, our lives went off in different directions. I decided I was going out into the world and seek my fortune. I joined the merchant marine. Saw the world all right but missed the fortune. Clement never left town except to get a college degree. He stayed here in Uromund, ran the little town newspaper, then surprised everybody by becoming a world-famous author, and rich in the process.

"A few years ago, I got tired of chasing rainbows and homesick for the hunting and fishing in the Big Thicket. So I came back. Clement offered me a job as caretaker on this big, elegant place of his. I've been here ever since."

Having finished his breakfast, he took a pipe from a

rack and fussed around, getting it lit. Deborah waited impatiently for him to continue his narrative about Clement Vaulkhurst. "My parents have told me a lot of family anecdotes about Clement," she said. "But I'm eager to hear firsthand what people around here think about him—his neighbors, the people he has contact with all the time."

Andrew Smith nodded. He puffed thoughtfully on his pipe and then said, "Clement is disliked by a lot of people because he has a way of poking into folks' lives. He has a great curiosity about human nature: what makes people behave the way they do. I think that may be one reason he's satisfied to go on living in this little town, though he could certainly afford to live anywhere in the world now. This town is like a laboratory for Clement. He puts all the people he knows in his mental test tube so he can study them—and later he writes about the way the human spirit functions. He sure knows all the secrets of Uromund. If there are any cheating wives, sticky-fingered bankers, or crooked political dealings, you can be sure Clement finds out about it. He has radar about stuff like that."

Andrew rubbed his pipe bowl against his jaw, looking at Deborah keenly. "For that reason, I have a hunch folks around here are not going to be very pleased about you poking around, asking questions about Clement. I'd watch my step carefully, young lady."

Deborah felt an unpleasant chill run up her spine. "Why on earth would they be angry with me?"

"Oh, it's just that they're touchy where Clement Vaulkhurst is concerned. They might think you're going to run across some of the old scandals Clement knew about and publicize them. They might think you're a newspaper reporter pretending to be a college girl writing a thesis. Everybody knows Clement is working on a new novel, and the whole town is jittery and scared about what he's coming out with this time. The folks here are searching through the old skeletons in their family closets and wondering if they're going to find themselves in his new book."

"I'll be careful," she said slowly. "It sounds as if Clement has made the whole town paranoid about him—kind of the way the citizens of Asheville, North Carolina, felt about Thomas Wolfe!"

"Well, they have mixed feelings. On the one hand, they're proud to have a hometown boy turn into such a famous writer. He put Uromund on the map, you might say. On the other hand, they don't like the way he keeps rattling those family skeletons."

They were silent for a moment, then Deborah asked, "By the way, who painted that portrait of Clement that hangs in his study? It's a remarkable piece of work." She felt her cheeks grow warm as she thought about the effect it had had on her.

"That was done by a woman artist, Serna Czerny. She came from Europe somewhere—Hungary, I think—a couple of years ago and set up an art studio in a city not far from here. She and Clement became . . . close friends. I don't think anyone else could have talked him into posing for a portrait."

Deborah felt a peculiar, biting emotion race through her. "When you say they are close friends, you mean she's his mistress, don't you?" she asked, surprised at the sharp note of anger in her voice.

The caretaker looked embarrassed. "I really don't know about that, Miss Deborah. They spend a lot of time together is all I know. I don't meddle in Clement's personal life."

"You don't have to defend him," she said coldly. "I know all about his reputation with women."

Deborah was surprised and confused by the flood of powerful emotions stirred up in her at the mention of Clement Vaulkhurst's mistress. What possible difference should it make to her that the woman was in love with him? She should not be surprised. Only someone on intimate terms with Clement, someone who knew his innermost soul, could have captured so vividly the essence of the man on canvas. The painting had obviously been done by an artist in love with her subject.

Deborah searched her own soul. This entire year she had been obsessed with Clement Vaulkhurst's writings. In her literature class, she had immersed herself in his novels and had fallen under the spell of his genius. And then she had come here and he had suddenly become a real person. Visiting the town where he lived, seeing the remarkable portrait, touching the desk where he wrote, and then coming face to face with him—it had all been a stunning emotional experience, one that had her totally confused.

She thought about that blazing moment last night when Clement had kissed her, and the shocking response in her body, the way every nerve end had tingled, the sudden rush of a carnal passion she had never dreamed of in her staid, conventional existence. Thinking about it now brought a sudden heat to her body and a flush to her cheeks.

Resolutely, she put those thoughts out of her mind and changed the conversation to a safer subject. "I want to talk to some more people around here who know Clement as well as you do. For added dimension when I write about him," she explained. "Do you have any suggestions?"

The caretaker thought for a moment, then said, "Well, you might go see old Barney Patterson. He worked for Clement when Clement published the weekly newspaper. The two of them ran the thing. Clement did the writing, and Barney set type and did whatever else it is you do to get out a weekly paper. Of course, after Clement got famous, he stopped fooling with the paper and spent all his time writing books. Barney took over the paper and runs it by himself now. Clement just handed him the keys one day and walked out. Gave it to him, lock, stock, and barrel. They're still good friends—drinking buddies, you might say. They often hang one on together at that beer joint down on the river, Indian Red's place. That's Clement's favorite watering hole." Andrew Smith nodded. "Yeah, I'd say old Barney could tell you some pretty good stories about Clement."

"Thanks." She smiled. "I appreciate the lead. And I certainly appreciate the hot tea and the breakfast. I feel almost human again."

"The pleasure is all mine," he said with a shy smile. "Don't have many pretty young ladies sample my cooking."

"You're a fine host, Andrew. And a real gentleman." *Which is more than I can say for your employer, Clement Vaulkhurst,* she added mentally.

The caretaker escorted her back to the main house. She planned to gather up her purse and leave at once before Clement returned.

But as she was hurrying to the front door, it opened, and she came face to face with the devil himself. And with him was a stunningly beautiful raven-haired woman.

"Well, if it isn't my little cousin!" Clement laughed in a baritone voice that seemed to make the windows rattle. "How's the head this morning, child? Pounding, no doubt!"

She raised her chin and gave him a cold stare. "My head is perfectly fine, thank you."

Clement chuckled, then turned to the woman beside him, who was regarding Deborah curiously. "Serna, this is the young lady I was telling you about, my kissing cousin, Deborah Denhoff. Deborah, this is Serna Czerny."

Deborah felt a peculiar cold shock at the unexpected meeting with Clement's mistress. She felt unnerved by the woman's intense beauty and commanding presence. At the same time she was embarrassed and furious at Clement's pointed emphasis on the phrase "kissing cousin." She wondered if the artist knew that Deborah had spent the night in this house alone with Clement. And she surmised, by the cool appraisal the beautiful dark-eyed woman was giving her, that she did, indeed, know all about last night.

Deborah had the distinct impression that Clement Vaulkhurst was cruel enough to have told the artist all about Deborah's visit and about the brandy, and probably embellished the facts. She remembered what Andrew Smith had said about Clement's "fabrications" and her mother's mention of his delight in playing monstrous jokes even if it meant using his creative imagination to embroider the truth.

She found her voice. "I'm pleased to meet you."

The artist made no move to shake hands. Clement, watching the two women, appeared to be enjoying the situation. "This young woman," he said to Serna, "is a college student who has the notion that she's going to write a thesis exposing my private life to the world." He seemed more amused now than angry.

Deborah glared at him. "I'm afraid I didn't pick a very appealing subject." To the artist, she said, "Good day, Miss Czerny. It was a pleasure meeting you. I want to compliment you on your artistic ability. That's a magnificent portrait of Clement in the study. You captured his conceit and meanness beautifully!"

She stormed out of the house with Clement's roaring laughter echoing in her ears.

Chapter Four

She was trembling with a mixture of emotions when she started her car and headed back to town. After a few miles, the predominent emotion—anger—faded, and she said aloud, "Deborah Denhoff, you *idiot!* How do you expect to get any cooperation out of that man if you insult him?"

And then she thought that any effort to insult Clement Vaulkhurst would probably bounce off like drops of water on an impervious surface. He simply didn't care what anyone else thought of him—especially Deborah Denhoff!

Next she asked herself, Do I really want to do this biographical thesis about Clement Vaulkhurst? The man is impossible. If this first meeting is a taste of what I'm in for, this is going to be the most miserable summer of my life. He's not only *not* going to be any help, he's going to insult and fight me all the way!

She remembered her parents' warning about Clement. Her father had said, "You may not like what you turn up. Clement is a strange man, not like other men.

Many people dislike him because of his independence and arrogance."

And her mother had warned, "You're not going to get much help from Clement. He'll probably be furious when he learns what you're doing. . . ."

Aloud, Deborah said, "What I really should do—if I have any brains at all—is throw my bags in the car and leave this place this morning . . . forget this whole idea." She was sure that Dr. Groves, the head of the English department, would allow her to change the subject of her thesis.

She was still debating the matter when she pulled under the grove of pine trees in the graveled parking area of the motel. She sat there for a few minutes, chewing on her inner lip and drumming her fingernails nervously against the steering wheel.

While her better judgment told her to flee this place at once, another side of her rebelled at giving up so easily. She became depressed at the consequences of leaving now. This project was to have been a symbol of her newly found independence, her emerging adult womanhood. To wave the white flag and go back home now would mean having to admit to her parents and Bill Hughbank that they were right, that this had been a harebrained scheme beyond her capabilities . . . that she wasn't really grown up or tough enough to hack it.

She sighed and shook her head. "Clement Vaulkhurst," she said through her teeth, "I can't let you do that to me. I can't give up this easily."

She thought that even if she couldn't get any cooperation from Clement himself, she could still do the thesis. She could research this town and talk with people who knew him, like the newspaperman Barney Patterson. She could go see Aunt Christina, who just might surprise her and allow her to borrow Clement's early diaries and journals.

With a surge of renewed determination, she stepped from her car and strode to her motel cabin. The first thing to do, she thought, was to take a good, hot shower. She felt gritty from the long drive yesterday and sleeping in her clothes last night.

The bath and a change of clothes did wonders for her morale. But then she caught sight of her image in the mirror. Suddenly Clement's appraisal of her echoed in her mind:

"If you got rid of those frumpy clothes and dowdy flat shoes and learned how to use makeup, you might even be attractive. . . ."

Hot tears rushed to her eyes. Was Clement's cruelly outspoken appraisal of her correct? Was that how she appeared to the world? It was true that she selected her wardrobe on the basis of functional practicality around the campus, and she used very little makeup. Her intellectual family was too concerned with activities of the mind to give much thought to external appearances. Her mother, who was color blind, had never made an effort to get Deborah to wear pretty clothes, and her father, who might as well have been color blind, couldn't have cared less. As far as her parents and siblings were concerned, clothes were simply a bothersome necessity. Deborah had never given the matter much thought until Clement's insulting remarks.

Suddenly, she clenched her fists. Furiously, she exploded. "Why do I let that man get under my skin this way?"

She put her feelings about him out of her mind and got busy with her portable typewriter, making preliminary notes for her thesis

At midmorning, there was a tap on her door. It was the motel owner, Doug Carpenter, attired in what appeared to be his standard uniform: scuffed boots, faded blue jeans, and a casual blue, short-sleeved shirt. He came bearing a pot of steaming coffee. "Compliments of the house. We try to keep our guests happy. We don't get many."

"How nice. I was just thinking I could do with a coffee break."

"Everything okay? Were you comfortable? Do you need more towels or anything?"

She smiled. "Everything is just fine."

"Don't forget, if you decide to stick around town for a while, I'll make a special rate by the week or month."

"Thanks," she said, accepting the steaming cup of coffee he poured for her. "I'll certainly keep it in mind."

He hesitated. "Mind if I sit down for a minute? I'll leave the door open so you won't be compromised."

"Now there's a lovely Victorian phrase. You're a gentleman of the old school, Mr. Carpenter."

He nodded toward her typewriter. "Looks like you've been busy."

"Yes, I have."

He poured himself a cup of coffee and carefully took a seat in one of the room's straight-back chairs. "I hear you drove out to Clement's place yesterday."

She felt a touch of annoyance. Was he prying or just making conversation? "Boy, small towns sure don't allow one much privacy, do they?"

"Not this one. But I guess you can understand why people here are curious. Pretty young city woman in a jazzy sports car drives into town all alone, just to come here and see Clement Vaulkhurst. People are bound to notice."

And I'm sure you wasted no time in spreading the word, Doug Carpenter, she thought, not sure if she should be amused or irritated.

"Well," she said, "it certainly is no secret why I'm here. As a matter of fact, I'd rather the entire town knew as soon as possible. It may help me get all the information I need. As I told you yesterday, I'm writing my master's thesis about Clement, so the more background I can get about him from the people in town, the more it will help me.

He took a sip of coffee. "Well, I was at the café last night. That's the local gossip nest. The theory making the rounds is that you're either a big-city newspaper reporter sent down here to get a story about Clement, or you're a lady detective."

Her mouth dropped open. "A lady *detective?* How glamorous."

He grinned. "It does have a kind of zing to it, doesn't it?"

"They won't buy the truth? That I'm just a college girl writing a thesis?"

He shrugged. "People around here are pretty touchy and suspicious about anything to do with Clement Vaulkhurst. The whole town nearly had a nervous breakdown that time the television people came to town to do an interview with him. Everybody gave a sigh of relief when he ran 'em off."

She grinned. "I heard about that. My mother said he sicced his dogs on them."

"That's the truth; he did."

Then she said, "Listen, Doug, you could help me. I

want to go see Christina Fallon today. Could you give me directions to her house?"

"Sure. Just take the street in front of the motel to the First Methodist Church, turn right at that corner, and go about six blocks. You can't miss her house. Big old two-story place with an iron fence around it. The house needs paint and the fence is rusty. Couple of those antique iron deer in the front yard. Ring the bell at the gate. If you try to walk into the yard without permission, there's a big, nasty Doberman that will chew you up."

"Good heavens! Thank you for warning me."

He nodded, then gathered up the coffeepot and empty cups. In the doorway, he paused. "I think Miss Christina is bedridden. At least, nobody has laid eyes on her in a year or more. She's got a housekeeper, a big, tough old gal, rough as a cob, named Hilda Balfour. Hilda is crazier than a bagful of lizards. She'd as soon sic her dog on you or shoot at you as look at you."

"Terrific," she said glumly. "I'm beginning to wonder why I ever came down here."

Deborah finished typing her preliminary notes. At noon she drove a few blocks to a hamburger place and had a light lunch. Then on to her great-great-aunt, Christina.

She found the house with no trouble. True to Doug Carpenter's warning, when she parked her car and walked up to the gate, the biggest, ugliest monster of a dog she had ever laid eyes on came bounding down from the porch, fangs dripping, growling and barking hysterically. When he leaped at the fence, snarling to get at her, the rusty enclosure rattled, and she wondered, with a feeling of panic, if the fence would hold.

She gave a jerk on the bell cord at the gate, and it set up a fearsome clanging. Presently, the front door opened a crack and a woman's voice bellowed out, "What d'you want?"

Over the noise of the raging dog, Deborah shouted back, "I want to visit Aunt Christina Fallon."

"Who're you? Why are you callin' her Aunt? You some kinda relative?"

It was a bit of a hair-raising situation, the dog clamoring to get through the fence to rip her limb from limb while the unseen woman in the house and Deborah screamed at each other over the ferocious barking.

"My name is Deborah Denhoff. My mother is Clement Vaulkhurst's cousin . . . sort of—"

The door slammed shut. She stood there, overwhelmed with frustration and dismay. But as she was about to turn away in defeat, the door opened a crack again. The dog suddenly behaved strangely. He stopped barking, pricked up his ears, whined, then turned and trotted meekly up to the porch. Deborah decided that the woman must be blowing one of those dog whistles that are pitched above frequencies audible to the human ear.

The black monster disappeared into the house. Then the woman called shrilly, "Well, come on, come on!"

Deborah hurried through the gate. The front door opened just enough for her to enter, then was slammed shut immediately. Her eyes, adjusting to the dim light inside the house, made out a large, raw-boned woman probably in her late fifties, dressed in a white uniform.

Beside the door was propped a murderous-looking shotgun. Deborah could see that Doug Carpenter had not been exaggerating about the Christina Fallon household.

"My name's Hilda Balfour," the woman said in a husky baritone. "I'm housekeeper and companion to Miss Christina. She's almost ninety, you know, and practically bedridden. She don't see nobody anymore— but you say you're kinfolk?"

"Yes." Deborah was glancing about uneasily for the dog, but he had disappeared somewhere in the back of the old house.

"Well, come along, then," the woman said grudgingly, leading the way up creaking stairs. She opened a door and ushered Deborah into a bedroom. An incredibly old and wrinkled woman attired in a white cotton nightgown was dozing in a wheelchair. The shades were drawn. The only light came from a dim bulb in a table lamp.

Mrs. Balfour gently shook Aunt Christina awake. "She came up to the gate," shouted the housekeeper, jabbing a thumb toward Deborah. "Says she's a relative."

Then Hilda Balfour explained, "You got to talk loud. The old woman's deaf as a post."

Christina Fallon looked at Deborah with clear eyes. "What are you after?" she demanded in the high-pitched, quavery voice of the very old. "I don't have any relatives."

"My name is Deborah Denhoff. My mother is Margaret Denhoff, your great-niece."

"You got to talk louder than that," the housekeeper warned.

"My mother was Clement's cousin," Deborah screamed.

The old woman sighed, her eyes becoming tearful. "Clement is always good to me. Some folks around here don't like Clement. They're jealous of his talent and his success. But he's like my own son. I adopted him when he was a boy, you know. Who did you say you were?"

"Deborah Denhoff," she yelled desperately. "My mother's maiden name was Margaret Fallon. She's your nephew Walter Fallon's daughter. She sent a letter—" Deborah fumbled in her purse for the note her mother had written to introduce her to Aunt Christina.

The old woman feebly removed a pair of silver-rimmed spectacles from a snap case on the table near her wheelchair and carefully fitted them over her ears. Then she studied the brief letter for a long time. When she leaned back, her eyes had a faraway expression. She seemed to forget that Deborah and Hilda Balfour were in the room as her mind lapsed into the past. Softly, she said, "Margaret comes to play with Clement often. She was here yesterday. They were climbing that tree in the back yard . . . some kind of game Clement thought up . . ." Her voice trailed off, and she appeared to doze.

Deborah looked around at the housekeeper, who shrugged and made an eloquent gesture, tapping her temple with her forefinger. Then she went over and shook Aunt Christina awake again.

"Well, what is it you want, child?" the old woman asked querulously.

Deborah drew a deep breath and shouted, "I would appreciate it very much if you would allow me to look through any old papers of Clement's that you might have. My mother said she thought you might have some diaries or journals he kept as a boy. Perhaps some letters of his. . . ."

Aunt Christina's eyes became troubled and suspicious. "What do want with those things? They're personal. . . ."

"I know. But I'm writing a college thesis about Clement. The whole world wants to know more about him. This kind of research is important. It means a great deal to me and to the literary world."

"I don't know. Those things are personal. I don't think Clement would like it."

"Please," Deborah begged. "Those things would help me write the truth about Clement. I'm going to do the thesis whether I have them or not—but they'd help me get the facts about him accurate. . . ."

"Well . . . " She frowned, then grumbled, "Since you're family, I guess it would be all right. Hilda, would you fetch that old box of Clement's things that we stored in the attic? Now stop pestering me, child. I'm tired, and I don't feel well." Her head slowly dropped forward as she dozed off again.

Deborah was leaving the room with the housekeeper when she was surprised by Aunt Christina's calling softly after her. "Clement thought a lot of your mother. She visited here many times when he was growing up. You give your mother my best regards, child."

The old woman's moments of lucidity were disconcerting. "Sane one minute, senile the next," muttered Hilda Balfour as she led the way to the attic.

As Deborah was leaving with the precious box of Clement's material clutched under her arm, Hilda Balfour told her, "You take real good care of that stuff.

I'm not sure if Mr. Vaulkhurst would want the old woman to be loaning it out. He pays me a good salary to look out after Aunt Christina and the house."

Deborah felt the housekeeper's cold, suspicious stare. She was certain the woman would waste little time in notifying Clement that Deborah had wheedled this box of memorabilia from his foster mother. What would his reaction be? she wondered uneasily. Probably fiery rage.

In her car, she opened her prize. She saw bundles of letters, journals scribbled in Clement's almost illegible scrawl, what looked like a short story that he might have written in high school, some faded snapshots.

She felt giddy with elation. No doubt, when she sorted through this material and deciphered Clement's handwriting, she was going to find some valuable gems for her thesis.

She decided that while she was on a winning streak, she'd better call on Barney Patterson, and she drove downtown to the office of the *Uromund Gazette*.

Barney Patterson, the weekly newspaper's publisher, editor, and printer, emerged from behind the clutter of an ancient printing press. He was an ink-stained gnome of a man who squinted at Deborah through smeared, gold-rimmed glasses.

"Hello," Deborah said. "Are you Mr. Patterson?"

"'Course I am. What can I do for you?"

"I'm Deborah Denhoff—"

"I know," he said impatiently, pushing his glasses back into place on the bony ridge of his nose with a grimy forefinger. "You're down here digging into Clement Vaulkhurst's life."

She gaped at him momentarily. "Well! For the second time today I find out that I'm an overnight celebrity in this town. Tell me, is there anyone in Uromund who doesn't know who I am and what I'm doing here?"

"I doubt it. Makes it a little discouraging printing a newspaper in this town."

His glasses were sliding down his nose again, and he pushed them back into place. "I guess you came to talk to me about Clement."

"Well, as a matter of fact, yes."

"Come on back here." He led the way around a maze of boxes, stacks of paper, and printing machinery to a small back room. The place smelled of paper, ink, and dust.

Deborah eyed the chair he offered her and realized her dress was going to the cleaner's if she sat in it, but she had no choice. The small-town newspaper man lowered himself into a creaking swivel chair, shoved his glasses back into place, opened the drawer of an ancient rolltop desk that would have driven an antique collector wild, and took out a brown bottle. "Scotch okay?"

"I beg your pardon?"

"Scotch. Is that okay with you? I might have some bourbon— Good heavens, don't tell me you're a teetotaler. I understood you were related to Clement."

"Oh . . . well, the Scotch will be fine."

"That's what Clement drinks. That or beer when we spend an evening at the honky-tonk on the river." Barney Patterson dug two tumblers from under a stack of papers, blew the dust out of one, half filled it with Scotch, and handed it to Deborah. "Sorry I haven't got any ice."

"That's all right," she said weakly, wondering if

Clement and his friends were conspiring to turn her into an alcoholic.

He half filled his glass, drank all of it, smacked his lips, refilled the glass, then settled back, propping his feet on the desk. He gave Deborah a thoughtful scrutiny. "You know, one of the stories circulating around town is that a big-city sensational tabloid has sent you down here to dig up a lot of dirt for an exposé about Clement's life."

She sighed. "Do I look like a newspaper reporter?"

"Hard to tell these days. Women's lib and all that. I just wouldn't want to see that kind of dirt printed about Clement. Oh, I'll admit, he does have his scandalous ways. But the man is a genius. And he always treated me fair. A lot of the rumors you hear about him are exaggerated, anyway."

"Mr. Patterson, my mother is Clement Vaulkhurst's cousin. I'm a graduate college student. Both my parents are on the university faculty. I'm simply here to gather biographical material for my master's thesis about Vaulkhurst's life. Now, you can easily check all this out—"

He waved his hand. "I believe you, young lady. I don't really put much stock in town gossip anyway. Your drink okay?"

She took a swallow of the warm Scotch, blinked back tears, and managed to say in a strangled voice that it was fine. Then she said, "Andrew Smith, the gardener and caretaker at Clement's estate, said that you worked with Clement when he had the paper. You must have known him pretty well."

"Oh, yes. You could say we're drinking buddies from way back."

Barney Patterson had another sip of Scotch. He leaned back in his chair and began to reminisce about the years he had been associated with Clement Vaulkhurst. But he had barely begun when a jangling bell at the front of the store announced the entrance of another caller. Patterson excused himself.

Deborah remained in the back room of the shop, nursing the drink of warm Scotch. She heard low voices at the front of the newspaper office but could not see who was talking to the printer or hear what was being said.

Presently the bell jangled again as the caller departed. Barney Patterson returned to the room where Deborah was waiting. His manner had undergone a sudden change. His relaxed, gossipy air had vanished, and now he was quite brusque. "I'm sorry, miss. I won't be able to talk to you anymore today. Just got a rush printing order."

With surprise and disappointment, Deborah protested, "But it wouldn't take long. We were just getting started—"

"Sorry."

"Well, can I call you tomorrow?"

Nervously, he put the bottle of Scotch back in the drawer and slammed it shut. "I'm going to be pretty busy getting out this week's newspaper. I'll call you when I get a breathing spell."

The next thing she knew, she was being ushered out of the shop. The door slammed behind her, and Deborah stood on the sidewalk, bewildered by the strange turn of events.

A car was pulling out of a parking space across the street, a sleek black Mercedes. It drove down the street

before Deborah had a clear view of the person behind
the wheel. Nevertheless, there was something familiar
about the driver.

Was it Clement Vaulkhurst? She was almost sure of
it. "So that was why Barney Patterson suddenly
clammed up!" she exclaimed. "Clement came by and
warned him not to talk to me. I'll bet that's what
happened."

At least she was glad she had gotten to Aunt
Christina before Clement had.

She returned to her motel room and spent the next
several hours eagerly sorting out the material she had
wheedled from Aunt Christina. So engrossed was she
with her absorbing task that she wasn't aware night had
fallen.

The sudden jangling of her telephone startled her.
She frowned at the instrument. Who on earth would be
calling her here? Gingerly she picked it up. "Yes?"

A familiar baritone voice rattled the earpiece. "Deborah, I want you to meet me right away. I have
something important to discuss with you."

"What is it?" she asked, angry at the commanding
manner in which Clement addressed her but piqued
with curiosity at the same time.

"I don't want to discuss it over the telephone."

She hesitated, gnawing at her lip. He probably
wanted to confront her in person to give her a
tongue-lashing for the way she had been prying into his
private life behind his back. She could do without that.

"I'm sorry," she said, "but I am very busy."

"So I've noticed," he said dryly. "However, it would
be distinctly to your advantage to stop whatever
piddling, totally inconsequential activity you are pres-

ently wasting your time on and meet me. I have a proposition to make to you—a *business* proposition—that I don't think you'll want to refuse."

How she wished she could tell him that nothing he could say to her would interest her and hang up. But he'd set her curiosity on fire.

"Meet me at the tavern on the river in a half hour," he commanded. "And if you don't know how to get there, ask Carpenter. I'm sure he's listening on the switchboard."

She heard a click as he hung up. She sat transfixed for a moment with frustrated fury at the presumptuous way Clement was ordering her around. "The conceit of that man!" she stormed.

Then she heard Doug Carpenter's voice on the line. "If you want to get to the tavern, go straight down the road in front of the motel for several miles to the river bridge. Indian Red's tavern is just across the bridge. You'll see a bunch of pickup trucks sitting around and hear some loud country-western music on the juke-box."

"You *were* eavesdropping!" she gasped.

"You can't call it eavesdropping if Clement figured I'd be listening," he said mildly.

She slammed the phone down, not sure if she was angrier with Clement or the motel owner. But no matter how angry she was, her curiosity was stronger. She found herself gathering up her purse and keys and going out to her car, muttering to herself the entire time.

The road out to the bridge turned out to be a rutted lane that took every bit of a half hour to navigate. Her sports car looked diminutive parked among the pickup trucks in front of the tavern. When she got out, she saw a pier jutting out over the river from the back of the beer joint. There was a shed beside the pier with a BAIT sign, and several flat-bottom boats were tied up on the river bank under great, moss-dripping oak trees. It was a typical east Texas river-bank establishment.

Doug Carpenter had been right about the pickup trucks and the jukebox. The music was tinny and loud. "Hemingway had Sloppy Joe's," she muttered, "and Clement Vaulkhurst has Indian Red's."

Nervously, she entered the smoke-filled tavern. She felt the curious glances of some tough-looking characters in blue jeans and scuffed cowboy boots at the bar, and then she met the brooding, dark-eyed stare of Clement Vaulkhurst, who was seated at a booth in a corner of the room.

She slid into the seat opposite the writer. He continued to fix a sullen glare on her. Finally, he said, "It's a good thing you're on time. I've ordered fried perch and hushpuppies. You have to eat them hot."

"What makes you think I'd want to eat?"

"Well, you've been so busy today running all over town digging into my personal life behind my back that I'm sure you've worked up a pretty good appetite."

"So that's why you wanted me to come out here—in order to chew me out. I thought as much. Well, you can just save your breath. I didn't drive out here over that miserable road for a lecture. This is still a free country, and I have a perfect legal right to interview whomever I wish. You don't make the laws in this city, Clement Vaulkhurst."

She started to rise, but he thundered, "Sit down. You are not going to insult me and the owner of this establishment by walking out on a meal he is taking extra pains to prepare!"

She gasped. "I don't believe this! You sound as if Indian Red is a temperamental French chef at some internationally known Parisian restaurant instead of a backwoods hick in a dirty apron leaning over a greasy frying pan!"

Clement scorched her with a black-eyed look. "I will overlook that infantile remark solely because it is the result of your hopeless naïveté and New England provincialism. For your enlightenment, Indian Red is known far and wide for his exquisite fresh-caught perch and his secret recipe for hushpuppies. You will judge for yourself in a few minutes."

He took a sip of his beer and continued, "As for my chewing you out, indeed I do plan to give you something of a tongue-lashing, young lady. I told you last night that I did not wish your amateurish efforts at being a biographer to embarrass me. Then I find out that you have pumped my gardener, stolen my material from my poor senile foster mother, and tried to give my ex–business partner the third degree about me—"

"I did not," she interrupted furiously, "'pump' your gardener. Mr. Smith very kindly made breakfast for me and simply began chatting about you entirely of his own volition. I didn't 'steal' anything from your foster mother. Aunt Christina very kindly lent me a box of memorabilia she had stored in the attic. And I didn't give Barney Patterson any 'third degree,' because you came by and shut him up!"

Vaulkhurst looked at her with a black eyebrow raised and gave a deep-throated chuckle.

"Incidentally, Andrew Smith said you're the biggest liar in Texas and I believe him!"

Vaulkhurst's chuckle turned into laughter.

"I suppose it is impossible to insult you," she

admitted. "And now that you have given me your so-called tongue-lashing, I am going. You may eat my order of Indian Red's nationally known hushpuppies or—or put them where you wish!"

For the second time she started to rise.

"Don't you want to hear my business proposition?" he asked, giving her a veiled look.

"No, I don't. I can well imagine what kind of business proposition you'd make me."

"Don't flatter yourself. I don't molest children."

"That does it," she said furiously. She stormed out to her car without a backward glance.

But when she tried to open the door, a big hand fell on it, keeping it closed. She spun around. Clement towered over her, a black, threatening silhouette in the darkness. He said, "You are about to pass up an opportunity that any number of writers would trade their mothers for. I'm going to offer to give you all the firsthand information you'll need for your biographical thesis. I'll even help you with it."

He had caught her totally off guard. For a moment she was speechless, then she spluttered, "But you've been furious at me for doing this. You're angry with me for trying to get personal information about your life. You called it an invasion of privacy."

"Indeed, it is just that," he admitted. "But I've been giving the matter a lot of thought. Now, obviously, you are a very stubborn young woman. You have this *idée fixe* that you are going to write your ridiculous thesis no matter what my feelings are about the matter. You'll wind up with a collection of half-truths and distortions about Clement Vaulkhurst that eager researchers will believe, pointing out that you are some kind of relative of mine and therefore must have inside information.

"I suppose I could sue you," he said, the darkness only half concealing his brooding expression. However, lawsuits are a waste of time; only the lawyers get rich from them. So, the only alternative is, as the saying goes, 'If you can't lick 'em, join 'em.' In our case, since I can't stop you from writing my biography, what I'd better do is see that you do a proper job of it."

She was stunned by the unexpected offer, so much so that she was unable to reply.

"What I'm offering is this," he continued. "As you may know, I am completing work on a new novel. I need some help with editing and typing the final draft. I propose that you come over and help me with the book, thus having the opportunity to see at first hand how Clement Vaulkhurst works. Along with that, we'll spend some time discussing my life, my philosophy, my concepts. In short, I am offering you the opportunity to become my Boswell. Then you can write up your rough draft of your biographical thesis. I'll take what will no doubt be a lot of awkward, incoherent scribbling and help you polish it into a final draft that will at least have some modicum of coherence and style. Now, what do you say to that, my little cousin?"

She couldn't say anything. She was struck speechless. This was truly the opportunity of a lifetime, and indeed countless writers would mortgage their souls to get such an open door to the private and jealously guarded life of Clement Vaulkhurst.

"Well, come on, come on. Make up your mind," he said impatiently. "Indian Red will be serving the perch and hushpuppies any minute, and we must not let them get cold."

"It's—it's a very tempting offer," she admitted weakly.

"Tempting? Good heavens, child, it's an offer no one in her right mind could refuse!"

Overlooking for the moment her irritation at his colossal ego, she said, "When would I start?"

"Right away. You can check out of that third-rate motel of Doug Carpenter's and into my guest room."

She looked at him warily. "You'd want me to move in with you?"

"I'd want you on the premises at all times. 'Moving in' with me implies some kind of cohabitation, which does not appeal to me at all."

She felt a sting of hurt pride. Tears rushed to her eyes. "I'm not appealing as a—a woman?" she stammered.

"Oh, I suppose to some college sophomore who has a larger supply of male hormones than discernment you might do for a romp in the hay after a rock concert. You do have a certain fresh young healthy physical appeal, but I prefer my women more sophisticated and less virginal."

Anger took the place of hurt feelings. "I'm glad to have you put it so bluntly. Now I can move into your guest room with no fear at all that sex will be part of your deal."

"Oh, I didn't say that you had nothing to fear in regard to losing your virginity. I said I don't have time to bother with anyone as uptight and conventional as you are. But sexual attraction is a two-way matter, you see. If you are working so close to me day after day, you will have your own desire to contend with. You may become so attracted to me that, if I should change my mind about you, you would succumb to me like that." He snapped his fingers.

Her eyes widened. She felt herself tremble with fury.

Through her teeth, she said, "You are absolutely incredible, do you know that? You have the conceit and ego of ten men. And the astounding thing is that you really believe what you just said. You think you could seduce me any time you wished!"

"I was merely trying to warn you—to put you on guard." He smiled. "You see, despite your stuffy conventional hang-ups, which I find terribly boring, and your total lack of understanding about what to do with your hair, how to use makeup, and what clothes to wear, I do detect a quality of determination and courage in you that I rather like. Now, I should further warn you that a worldly, experienced man like me can derive quite a bit of sexual satisfaction out of corrupting someone fresh and young and innocent like you. A moment ago I said that I would not find a liaison with you appealing, that I preferred my women less hide-bound by convention and more sophisticated. However, I'll contradict that to some extent by saying that it would be rather exciting to teach you the ways of love, to see your defenses and inhibitions crumble, to turn you from a pallid, stuffy young spinster into a writhing, panting woman consumed by passion, doing things in bed with a man that you only dream about in your most secret fantasies."

Deborah's cheeks grew hot, and her heart pounded with a strange and unbidden force. "You *are* a devil."

"Perhaps," he said with a sly smile. "And, as such, I could appeal to your baser instincts. The needs and desires buried somewhere under your veneer of civilized inhibitions would respond to my needs and desires. With another man you might feel obliged to keep up your pretense of modesty and chastity. With me, since you despise me to begin with, and since you consider me the embodiment of evil, you would have nothing to lose by plunging to the depths of animal passion."

"I—I won't listen to any more of this," she gasped, hating herself for the strange, dark excitement he was stirring in her. Was he some kind of Svengali, putting her under his evil hypnotic spell?

"Don't delude yourself," he murmured, moving a step closer to her. "Under that cold alabaster exterior of yours, there lie slumbering all the instincts of womankind hungering for sexual experience. Our civilized veneer is quite thin indeed. One does not have to scratch very deep to find raging primitive passions. Courtesans, seductresses, scarlet women—they are your sisters, my dear, and more closely related than you might think."

He was so close now that she could feel the heat from his body. Her heart was pounding wildly, and her legs had become weak, her mouth dry. She was terrified and repulsed by him, and at the same time perversely and powerfully attracted.

"Yes," he continued, "a night in bed with me would open to you a world of pleasure that you have never dreamed of. I could kiss you into submission, teach you delights that would make you gasp and swoon, make love to you for hours, and carry you to one mountain-top after another of fulfillment."

His face was very close now. She could not tear her gaze from his dark eyes. They seemed to be black pools of violence that were sucking her into their bottomless vortex. Her dry lips parted, but she could not speak. She was transfixed with terror and attraction, like a moth coming ever closer to the fatal flame.

There was a faint smile of self-assurance on his lips. His powerful arms encircled her. Then she was very close to him, her bosom pressed tightly against his broad, powerful chest.

His mouth came down on hers with a searing flame that ignited her entire body. She was shocked, dismayed, immobilized at first. When she could marshal her scattered senses, she struggled, trying to wrench from his grasp. But she was helpless against his powerful muscles.

She hated the part of her that was responding to him—hated it, fought it . . . and lost. She closed her eyes and drowned in the ecstasy of the moment.

Vaguely she was conscious of his hand expertly opening the buttons at the front of her dress. She shuddered as the hard flesh of his fingers hunted under her bra and found the tender secrets of her breasts.

That invasion of her private person was a cold shock that brought her back to sanity and reality. It gave her the strength to pull away from him.

"No," she said. "No . . . no . . . no—"

She quickly closed the buttons, facing him disheveled but with chin raised and voice firm. "You are quite right, Clement. I do have the potential to be the passionate, abandoned woman you described. But you will never find out. Sorry to damage your colossal ego. You're not the man who will know me. Perhaps I am stuffy and conventional. Those are my values. They are what make me a civilized person with moral standards and self-respect. You certainly can arouse me physically—you just demonstrated that. But I can still set limits on my desire. When I cross those limits, it will be with a man who is my husband, who plans to take care of me and cherish me and remain at my side for the rest of my life. Now, I'm sorry if that sounds hopelessly old-fashioned and square—" She caught herself, and her eyes blazed. "No, I'm *not* sorry. Why should I apologize for having some values I'm proud of?"

He was regarding her with an expression that was amused and at the same time slightly puzzled. "Bravo! That was quite a speech for a schoolgirl. Perhaps there is more to your character than I suspected—dull and predictable though it may be."

Then he said, "Well, now that we have all that out of our system, what is your decision in regard to being my houseguest and accepting my help with your biographical thesis? Do you still wish to do it, or was that little speech you just made your refusal on the grounds that it violates your stuffy conventionality?"

"You miss the point," she said coldly. "I was talking about my own personal view of myself and the value I place on myself. It has nothing to do with the usual definition of conventionality. All my life I have been hemmed in and stifled because I felt I must do what people expected of me. I'll be frank, Clement, and admit that I really envy your ability to go through life not caring what people think about you. It's a quality I would like to acquire. It must give one a tremendous sense of freedom. I can't help but admire you for that."

He raised an eyebrow. "Glory be—you have actually found something about me of which you approve."

"Don't let it go to your head," she said grimly. "It's far outweighed by things of which I disapprove."

They eyed each other in silence for a moment, then both broke into grins.

"Well, now that we have cleared the air and understand what we dislike about each other, can we be friendly enemies?" He chuckled.

"I suppose. At least for as long as it takes for me to finish the thesis. Yes, I do intend to take up your offer.

I'd be an idiot to refuse—as you pointed out. This could be a tremendous achievement for me. I will be your houseguest, and I'll show my appreciation by working hard."

"You realize that people in town will be convinced you've moved in with me to become my mistress. The gossip may even reach back to your home. The tabloids would love to pounce on a juicy tidbit like that."

She shrugged. "Let me deal with that in my own way. I told you I'm trying to get out of this straitjacket of conventionality that has stifled me so much of my life."

"Good for you. Now, shall we partake of the delicious meal that will be waiting for us inside?"

He offered her his arm and gallantly escorted her back into the tavern.

Inwardly, she felt a lot less self-assured that she appeared on the surface. Doubts and fears assailed her. What was she letting herself in for? She looked up at the dark, powerful, enigmatic man beside her. Who knew what he was capable of? What kind of dangers awaited her in Clement Vaulkhurst's home? She felt a sense of foreboding that sent a shiver through her. He had given her a warning. Was she a fool to disregard it? Was she really as strong as she thought? Tonight he had given her a demonstration of how powerful his physical appeal could be. Would that attraction become overwhelming if she was around him day after day?

A small voice of sanity warned her that what she should do was get in her car at once and put all the distance she could between herself and Clement Vaulkhurst.

Chapter Five

Deborah removed a sheet of paper from her typewriter, reread what she had just typed, and placed it atop the growing stack on her desk. She leaned back and slowly rubbed the fatigue from the back of her neck. She had been typing since early this morning, and a wave of weariness assailed her.

The neat pile of typed pages beside her typewriter was the product of the week she had been helping Clement Vaulkhurst complete the final draft of his new novel. She stared at it with a feeling of unreality that still haunted her. She still found it hard to believe that she had been rash enough to accept Clement's proposition and move into his guest room. It had been a daring, unconventional adventure, totally out of character for her.

The day she moved out of the motel, Doug Carpenter had tried, in his affable way, to dissuade her. As he carried her bags to her car he had warned, "You're a super-nice young lady, Miss Deborah. I hope you'll pardon me for saying this, but I get the impression you've led a pretty sheltered life. I wonder if you really understand what kind of a reputation Clement Vaulkhurst has."

She had smiled at the motel owner. He had irritated her at times with his prying, gossipy manner. But basically he was a pretty nice guy, and she'd decided she liked him. "I may have led a sheltered life, Doug, but I'm over twenty-one, and I do know all about the birds and the bees and the facts of life. Yes, I know Clement is something of a devil with women. But don't worry about me. I know him for what he is, and I'm perfectly capable of taking care of myself."

Carpenter had looked at her with troubled eyes. "I'm sure you are. But you ought to know that this town is going to rip you into little pieces when folks find out that you've moved in with Clement. Your reputation won't be worth a plugged nickel. You might as well prepare yourself to be stared at and hear snickers behind your back when you come to town. You'll be known around here as Clement's new live-in mistress."

Deborah had blushed, more dismayed by his words than she let him see. "It's—it's not important to me what these provincial, small-town people think. I don't know any of them personally. I'll be gone at the end of summer, and I'll never see any of them again."

"That's true. But don't count on the gossip staying in the city limits. Clement Vaulkhurst is a national news item. His carryings-on usually make the tabloids. Somebody is bound to spread the news about his latest girl friend, and one day you're going to walk into a grocery store and see yourself looking back from the cover of a gossip magazine."

Deborah had felt genuine dismay at that warning. It had been a possibility she'd tried to push out of her mind. Doug's putting it into words had made her face the danger. What if her parents or the university faculty back home or Bill Hughbank read such a lurid, distorted gossip story, linking her and Clement Vaulkhurst in such a sordid fashion?

A good measure of her newly declared independence had faltered. But she thought about the fabulous opportunity she'd have, working so close to one of the world's most eminent novelists, and receiving his direct assistance with her biographical assistance. How could she pass up such an offer?

The answer was, of course, that she could not. This was the chance of a lifetime, and she must seize it, come what may.

Now, after spending a week as Clement's house-guest, she did not regret one bit her decision. The impact of actually playing a firsthand part—small though it might be—in the final draft of a Vaulkhurst novel was breathtaking. As much as she despised him, she was awed by his genius. As before, she fell under the spell of Clement Vaulkhurst the novelist, while she scorned Clement Vaulkhurst the man.

Despite her misgivings, during this first week she'd encountered no personal danger in such close daily proximity to Clement. His entire personality changed when he was working. He seemed to detach himself completely from any physical needs. His intense con-centration was remarkable. He drove himself with a kind of relentless inner fury. He withdrew into a dark, brooding shell that had little contact with objective existence. He appeared to eat practically nothing, existing completely on a burning inner creative force. Sleep consisted of occasional catnaps on the couch in his study. Deborah woke several times at various hours of the night to hear his typewriter pounding furiously down in his study.

He made no romantic passes at her. Far from it. Most of the time he appeared unaware of her existence. When he did notice her, he did little more than snarl at her.

It was in some ways a nerve-racking situation, and yet exciting. Anything Deborah had done before paled into trivia compared to this experience. She was a firsthand participant in the creation of a great work of literature, one that might well endure for centuries. She could only be grateful to a kind fate for this opportunity.

Then, this morning, a startling change had come over Clement. He suddenly tossed aside a page he was working on, stood up, and stretched. He looked like a sleepwalker emerging from a trancelike stage. With a muttered curse, he threw all the pages he'd been working on into a desk drawer and stalked out of the room. In a short while, she heard the shower running furiously upstairs in his room, heard him bellowing some kind of ribald barroom song off key. She heard him yell out of a window for Andrew Smith to come scramble him a half dozen eggs; he was starved.

An hour later, he strode into the study where Deborah was typing. He was shaved, dressed in sharply creased white linen trousers and a crisply pressed blue silk shirt. He was carrying a drink in one hand.

"Enough of this ridiculous work," he said heartily. "I'm going to spend a few days playing. Why don't you take a holiday, too, little cousin?"

"Well, I want to finish typing this chapter."

"Suit yourself. Such dedication to work bores me. I'm off to have a little fun."

"Clement," she said, looking at him earnestly. "I—I don't know exactly how to say this. I want you to know how inspiring it has been to work with you this week—and how much I appreciate this opportunity you've given me. . . ."

"Nonsense," he snorted. "Don't go getting maudlin on me. I'm not going out of my way to give you anything. You're earning your way. You've been a big help."

Without warning, he suddenly reached around and gave her a firm squeeze and a pat.

Red-faced, she jumped back out of reach with an angry gasp.

He grinned. "Very nice. Firm, compact, yet well rounded."

"Listen, you keep your hands to yourself," she spluttered.

He only laughed at her disconcertedness. He raked her figure from head to toe with a bold, appraising stare that made her blush to the roots of her hair. "Y'know, little cousin, you actually have a remarkable body under those dowdy clothes and spinsterish librarian exterior. I think I'll speak to my artist friend Serna Czerny about painting you nude sometimes."

"You'll do no such thing!" she cried. "I'm not—I wouldn't . . . not in a million years!"

"Hogwash! There isn't a woman alive who wouldn't secretly like to have herself painted or photographed in the nude. That is, unless she's flat-chested or overweight. And you are neither of those."

Deborah glared at him. "Well, I can see the nasty side of you has emerged again. This past week I was actually beginning to form some respect for you."

He merely laughed in his infuriating manner and

strode out of the room, leaving her shaking with anger and frustration. In a few minutes, she heard his car pull out of the driveway.

She thought, *The man is totally without scruples or decency!*

It took her a half hour and two strong cups of tea to pull herself back together after the upsetting encounter with the infuriating side of Clement Vaulkhurst. Finally, her trembling calmed down and she returned to her work. She typed in a frenzy, unleashing her anger on the typewriter keys.

She paused at noon only long enough to gulp down a sandwich, then threw herself back into her work. She became so engrossed in her task that she forgot all about her confrontation with Clement that morning. Then, at three o'clock, she heard his car return. She heard the front door open and close, then voices in the hallway—Clement's and a woman's.

She glanced up. Clement was standing in the study doorway, his arm around the waist of Serna Czerny.

"Still at it, little cousin?" Clement said in his rumbling baritone.

The woman beside him was directing a smoldering, measuring gaze at Deborah, who became self-conscious and ill at ease in the presence of the strikingly beautiful artist. Deborah realized that Serna Czerny must be quite aware of the new living arrangements in Clement's household, and she must be furious. But she was far too experienced a woman to expose her anger to Clement. Deborah, however, also being a woman and the object of Serna's fury as well, could see quite plainly the look of murder in the other woman's eyes.

Deborah could understand and sympathize. She hoped that she would have the opportunity to reassure

Serna Czerny that she had no designs on Clement. How could he be so cruel to his mistress? She obviously loved him. He must know how upsetting it was to her for him to bring Deborah into his home as his guest.

"Come along, my dear," Clement said to the artist. "Let us not interfere with the labor of my industrious little typist."

He gave the beautiful, dark-haired woman a fond squeeze around her waist and led her off.

Deborah heard their voices fade away. She heard a door close somewhere upstairs. Then all was quiet.

She tried to return to her work, but her concentration was shot. Her thoughts persisted in straying to the couple upstairs. She visualized them together, Serna locked in Clement's arms in a passionate embrace . . . saw them making love. . . .

Her cheeks burned. She crumpled up a sheet of paper into a tight ball and hurled it at the wall. How dare Clement bring his mistress here for an afternoon of lovemaking! Had he no shame at all, no sense of decency?

The more Deborah thought about what was going on upstairs behind the closed door, the more furious she became. The storm of emotions that had been stirred up in her by the situation both confused and upset her. She couldn't understand why she was so disturbed. She only wished they had gone somewhere else for their clandestine lovemaking.

She gave up trying to work altogether. For a while she paced around the study like a caged animal. She felt her cheeks. They were hot.

She thought about the generous-sized swimming pool back of Clement's mansion. Suddenly, the cool blue water was very inviting.

She put a cover on the typewriter and hurried up to the guest room, where she changed into a sleek, form-fitting white bathing suit that she had fortunately packed with her other garments. She turned before a full-length mirror. The back of the suit was cut daringly low and bare except for thin straps crisscrossing between her shoulder blades. It revealed her slim, firm young figure. She remembered what Clement had said about her qualifications as an artist's model. She slammed out of the room.

Downstairs, she plunged into the pool with a smooth, expert dive. She was a good swimmer. The water churned as she crossed and recrossed the pool with fast strokes.

Her pent-up emotions spent at last, she floated on her back, gazing up at the cloud-flecked blue sky. She remembered how, as a child, she could spend hours on a grassy hill, watching the shapes of puffball clouds parade across the sky.

Suddenly, a dark figure intruded on the perimeter of her vision. She turned her head abruptly. Clement Vaulkhurst stood on the edge of the pool, watching her.

He was dressed in dark swimming trunks. In the first surprised moment, she could only admire his superb physique. Powerful muscles rippled across his broad shoulders and deep chest. He was a big man all over, tall, strong, and yet without an ounce of excess fat. His waist was tight and firm. The muscles in his thighs were like steel ropes. He was burned a handsome bronze by the Texas sun.

He said, "You have a very nice form, little cousin."

She lost her floating position and floundered in the water for a moment until she regained her equilibrium, treading water now.

"You are referring to my swimming, of course," she spluttered.

He arched an eyebrow. "Oh, of course." He chuckled.

"You shouldn't sneak up on a person that way. You startled me."

"Sorry. I wasn't aware that I was sneaking up on you. You appeared to be in some sort of reverie when I walked up. That's why you didn't hear me. Were you daydreaming about the boyfriend back home?"

"Perhaps," she said coldly. "Though I fail to see how it is any concern of yours."

He merely laughed at her. Then he dove into the water and, with a few powerful strokes, came up to her. "I heard you splashing around out here. It sounded like just the thing to do on a hot summer afternoon."

She backed away from him until her back was pinned against the side of the pool. Her feet touched bottom. "Is your friend Serna coming?"

"No, I don't think so. She doesn't have a bathing suit with her. And I don't think your conventional nature would permit skinny-dipping."

He chuckled at her discomfiture.

"Well, you may have the pool to yourself," she said coldly. "I'm getting out."

But he had moved closer to her and now faced her, trapping her with a powerful arm on each side, reaching around her to grip the edge of the pool. "No hurry, is there?" He smiled, his lips dangerously close to her mouth. "It's so cool and peaceful here." His voice had a deep, mesmerizing tone as his eyes held her magnetically.

She felt a warm flush creeping up her throat. What a beast he was—to come from the bed of his mistress straight down here to flirt with her! Didn't he have a shred of principle? Her body felt rigid. With an effort, she tore her gaze from his hypnotic eyes and looked around for a way to escape.

He was so calm, so relaxed, so self-assured. Darn him for that! she thought. And at the same time she was envious. Her emotional state was quite the opposite from his. She felt self-conscious, completely unsure of herself, and rattled.

Under the water, his body moved closer to hers. She felt the touch of his muscular thighs against her bare legs. Her breathing became shallow and fast. She marveled at the fiery flash of desire that ran shivering through her body.

His lips brushed hers, then came back to linger.

"No," she whispered against his mouth. "No . . . no . . ."

But his arm slipped below the surface of the water and encircled her waist, pulling her close to him. Their bare legs entwined. The desire that raged in her was almost out of control. Her pulse became a hammering drumbeat.

How could he do this? How could he come fresh from the arms of his paramour and kiss her like this? And, more to the point, how could she respond with such shameful abandon? And yet she couldn't will herself to tear her lips from his. Her body was limp.

It was a long kiss that shook her to the depths of her being. When it ended at last, his black eyes had the look of a conqueror. A faint smile tugged at his lips. "I warned you, little cousin," he teased softly. "I'm afraid your chastity hangs by a very thin thread."

Her bosom was rising and falling swiftly, the emotions he had awakened in her still rampant. But she met his look with her own gaze of defiance. "It's a very strong thread," she retorted. "And one that will never be broken by you!"

With that, she escaped his embrace, swam furiously to the opposite side of the pool, and pulled herself out. She jumped to her feet and grabbed her beach towel from a poolside table. As she wrapped the large towel around her, she glanced up at a second-story window. A face was looking down at her—the face of Serna Czerny, now stark white with rage.

Chapter Six

"That was quite a romantic scene in the pool."

Serna Czerny's voice had the quality of splintering icicles. Her gaze was coldly analytical, sizing up Deborah with the measuring look of a jealous woman.

Deborah had hurried from the pool to her room, where she had taken a quick shower and changed into a casual dress before the knock came at her door. She was dismayed at this embarrassing confrontation with Clement's artist friend. She had been ill at ease around the woman before the incident in the swimming pool. Now she was painfully humiliated.

As Serna Czerny moved into the room, she took a cork-tipped cigarette from a jacket pocket, touched a flame to it from a gold lighter, and inhaled deeply. She moved to a window, gazed out for a moment, then turned to face Deborah again. She spoke with a trace of an accent. "You're being quite foolish, you know."

Deborah clutched her comb, at a loss to know how to respond to the glamorous, sophisticated woman. She had to explain to Serna that what had happened in the pool had meant even less than nothing to her. "Miss Czerny—" she began.

But the artist made an impatient gesture with the hand holding the cigarette, interrupting Deborah. "It is no surprise that you would become enamored of Clement Vaulkhurst."

Deborah's eyes widened. *"Enamored!"*

"Of course. Please don't bore me with a ridiculous denial. Clement is, after all, an experienced, worldly, attractive man. And he can be devilishly charming. Just the combination to sweep a young, naïve woman off her feet. I am quite aware that you have moved in here with him."

"But—"

"The whole affair is most dreary. It's so trite. Dewy-eyed college coed swoons in the arms of the romantic Clement Vaulkhurst. Tell me, do you fancy yourself in love with him?"

Deborah's embarrassment was being replaced with a flush of anger. "Now, just a darn minute—"

"Because if you do, it's a pity for you, my dear. You seem a respectable enough young woman. Clement will leave you precious little self-respect when he's through with you. He's quite a villain where women are concerned, you know. He'll use you for his own selfish pleasure as long as he is amused, and then toss you aside. How tragic for your romantic schoolgirl illusions. I should warn you that a sheltered, naïve young thing like you is not emotionally equipped to handle an affair with Clement Vaulkhurst. You're playing in the big leagues, my child."

Any sympathy Deborah had felt for Serna Czerny evaporated in the heat of her rising anger. Furiously, she said, "I don't understand why you think you have the right to come up here and deliver a lecture to me. And I'm not your 'child'!"

"Well, you *are* a child, a babe in the woods with a man like Clement. I didn't come here to deliver a lecture. Rather, what I have to say is more in the nature of a warning. If you know what's good for you, you'll pack your bags and go back to your classroom."

"I have no intention of doing that!" Deborah exclaimed, white-lipped with fury now. "You can't order me around. I am here as Clement's houseguest. Only he can order me to leave. And as for your 'warning,' you don't scare me, Miss Czerny."

The older woman gave her a deadly stare. "You'd better shed some of your romantic illusions and listen to some facts. You are heading for an emotional catastrophe. Clement needs a highly intelligent, unconventional, and sophisticated woman to hold him. You are entirely too naïve, too much of a conformist, too hidebound by convention, to ever fit into Clement's life and make him happy or satisfy him. He'll become bored with you in record time. Then you'll be left to nurse your wounds . . . not a pleasant prospect for you."

Deborah was aware of the irony of the situation: Serna Czerny was obviously a woman beside herself with jealousy—and for absolutely no reason. Deborah was not only not having an affair with Clement, she didn't want him, wouldn't have him as a gift!

But the artist's words had stung deeply. When she accused Deborah of being conventional, stuffy, and a hidebound conformist, she had struck a raw nerve.

It was an assessment Deborah had once made of herself, and she had cringed. She was doing her best now to break out of the shell that had stifled her for so many years. She did not appreciate having Serna Czerny describe her in such unflattering terms. The woman's open hostility aroused her to a counterattack.

Rebelliously, she exclaimed, "You don't have the faintest notion what kind of a person I am, Miss Czerny. You might be surprised. I'm not quite the stuffy, conventional little square you make me out to be. I moved in here, didn't I, in spite of what the gossips might be saying about me. *That's* hardly being hidebound by convention! And I'm not quite as dumb and naïve as you seem to think, either. I'm thoroughly aware of Clement's reputation with women. You're not the first person to warn me about that. Doug Carpenter made it clear that if I moved out here, my reputation would be shot. But I'm not worried about that. It's something I made my own decision about and will deal with in my own way. As for what is going on between Clement and me, that is my own private matter!"

Deborah paused for breath, surprised at her outburst. She hadn't expected that she was capable of standing her ground so firmly before a woman like Serna Czerny. She suddenly felt proud of herself. And, hearing her thoughts put into words, she realized she had made some major decisions on her own for the first time in her life. It was an exhilarating feeling.

She knew she could very easily mollify Serna's jealousy and rage. It would be easy to cringe before the strong-willed artist, to meekly reassure her that she had no designs on Clement, that for this past week he had treated her like a piece of the furniture, and that that kiss in the swimming pool was the only romantic encounter they'd had—and it was not going to be repeated, if she had any say in the matter.

But Serna's hostile, superior attitude had awakened

a stubborn, rebellious streak in Deborah. Let her stew in her own juice, she thought. If she's made up her mind there's something going on between Clement and me, that's her problem! Until she's nicer to me, she can just go on being jealous.

The two women glared at each other across the room. Deborah sensed it was going to be open warfare between them. Well, she hadn't asked for it, but she was accepting the challenge.

Serna Czerny suddenly stabbed out her cigarette in an ashtray with a fierce gesture and stalked from the room.

Deborah collapsed on her bed, shaken by the encounter. She stared at the ceiling, playing over in her mind the dialogue with Serna Czerny. The angry scene had upset her, but it did have some amusing aspects. Serna—murderously jealous because she thought Deborah was stealing Clement away from her! A mischievous giggle tugged at Deborah's lips. How wrong could the woman be! Still, there were flattering overtones to the situation. That a beautiful, cosmopolitan, self-assured woman like Serna Czerny could be so jealous of her was no small boost to Deborah's ego.

Deborah grinned. Thank you, Serna, she said in her mind. You didn't know it, but you paid me quite a compliment.

If Serna hadn't been so hateful, Deborah would have been sympathetic. Jealousy was a painful emotion. But after today's encounter, Deborah knew she had a deadly enemy in Serna Czerny.

Well, she thought, as long as I'm Clement's house-guest, I'm sure he won't let Serna do anything violent. At the same time, he's such a rascal he's probably enjoying her being jealous over him—and is no doubt adding fuel to the fire in his own way, maybe even hinting that he's having a romantic fling with me! But I'm not going to lose any sleep over the situation. . . .

As if to demonstrate her resolve, Deborah drifted off into an afternoon nap. The week of hard work followed by the exertion of swimming and the emotion-packed encounters with Clement and then Serna had left her exhausted. She slept away most of the afternoon.

When she awoke, dusk was falling. The mansion was silent. She yawned and stretched, then rose and went to the window. From here she had a view of the grounds and the driveway. Clement's Mercedes was gone. Deborah gave a sigh of relief. She didn't think she was up to any more encounters with either Clement or his lady friend today.

She went downstairs to the kitchen, where she put together a bacon-and-tomato sandwich and poured a glass of cold milk. The telephone rang. She answered on the kitchen extension.

A familiar voice said, "Deborah? Is that you?"

She stared wide-eyed at the phone cradle. "Bill? Bill Hughbank? Wh—where are you?"

"I'm here in Uromund. I flew into Houston this afternoon and rented a car."

"You—you did?" was all she could think of to say.

"Yes. I've missed you like the dickens, Deborah. And I've been worried about you. I haven't heard one word from you."

She floundered mentally, trying to think of a logical explanation for why she hadn't written him. She'd fully intended to, each day, but somehow had put it off.

"Deborah, are you there?"

"Yes—forgive me, Bill. I'm just so surprised I can't think what to say. I had no idea you were coming down here."

"Well, I didn't call to let you know I was coming, because I had no idea how to get in touch with you." He sounded hurt and more than a little accusing.

"I've—I've been here at Clement's place. He's hired me to help him with the final draft of his new novel . . . and he's going to help me with my thesis. . . ."

There was a moment of uncomfortable silence. Then Bill said, "Well, I know. I mean, I know *now*. The fellow who runs this motel I checked into told me where you are. He seems to know all about you."

"Doug Carpenter? Are you at his place?"

"Yes."

She thought she would like to do physical harm to Doug Carpenter.

"Deborah, we need to have a talk. I'm coming out there."

"No," she said quickly. Then she said, "You—you may have trouble finding your way. I'll drive in to where you are. I'll leave right away. . . ."

She hung up, then sat on a kitchen stool, her knees feeling weak.

Chapter Seven

Deborah's mind was in turmoil as she drove to Doug Carpenter's motel. What else was this day going to bring?

She was totally unprepared to face Bill at this point. Perhaps that was why she hadn't written to him. Subconsciously, she had put all thoughts and emotions about Bill Hughbank on the back burner. She'd wanted this summer for herself, free of her life back home. Bill symbolized the things she was struggling with: her relationship with her family, the confines of the cloistered university life, all the predictable, stereotyped behavior patterns that Bill expected of her.

Before she had to face her feelings about Bill, she'd wanted to come to grips with her own metamorphosis. She felt a new individual emerging within her, an adult capable of making decisions, taking command of her own life. She'd wanted to become better acquainted with her new self, to explore its meaning, perhaps to take a few risks and taste life more completely on her own terms. By the end of summer, she expected, she'd know her own mind where Bill was concerned. She might decide that she loved him and did very much want to marry him. But it was not a decision she wanted to make at this point.

Darn you, anyway, Bill, she fumed. Why did you have to pick such an inopportune time to pay me a surprise visit?

She pulled into the graveled driveway of the motel. It was an easy matter to pick out the cabin occupied by Bill Hughbank.

Deborah parked beside Bill's rented sedan. She switched off her engine and sat for a moment, staring at the door, nervously tapping her steering wheel. How was she going to explain being Clement's houseguest? Bill wasn't going to like that even a little bit, she thought uneasily.

She mustered her courage, slid from behind the steering wheel, and went up to the door. It opened on her first timid knock. Bill stood silhouetted in the doorway. With the light behind him, Deborah couldn't see his face clearly.

"Deborah!" He stepped out to embrace and kiss her.

She quickly moved out of his arms. "Not here, Bill," she stammered self-consciously. "This little town is full of gossips."

They went inside, and Bill said, "Since when have you become so concerned about gossips?"

She shot him a questioning look, though with a sinking heart she knew full well what he meant.

"The guy who runs this motel—Doug Carpenter—appears to be one of your most active town gossips. I'd barely signed the register before he was giving me the third degree about who I was and what I was doing here. When I told him I was your boyfriend, he was only too eager to fill me in on your carryings-on."

"My *carryings-on* . . .?"

"Yes. You and this Clement Vaulkhurst fellow. Carpenter told me you'd moved in with Vaulkhurst. Deborah, I don't know what to say!"

It was now obvious to Deborah that under his surface of cool, rigid self-control Bill was fuming mad. She said, "I haven't 'moved in' with Clement. Not in the sense you seem to be implying. He invited me to spend several weeks as his houseguest while he finishes his novel and then helps me with the biographical thesis. It's a perfectly respectable arrangement, in spite of what Doug Carpenter and his gossipy neighbors might be saying."

"Respectable?" Bill arched an eyebrow. "Are you chaperoned?"

"Chaperoned?" she echoed, looking at him blankly. "Well, no . . . but there is a caretaker on the grounds." She added, with a touch of exasperation, "Bill, I'm a grown woman. An adult. And Clement is a relative—"

"A relative? A relative? I don't call a second or third cousin twice removed—and not even a blood relation at that—a relative."

Deborah felt all of her newfound independence and self-assurance dissolving in the face of Bill's anger with her. She was becoming flustered and defensive. She was actually feeling guilty, as if she now had to somehow prove her innocence.

Her face flushed, she said, "I don't care what kind of nasty rumors Doug Carpenter and his gossipy friends are spreading around. I haven't done anything wrong. It's a business arrangement, nothing more. Clement works at all hours, and he needs me on the premises.

It's been a wonderful opportunity for me, one I simply could not pass up. Do you realize that no definitive biography has ever been written about Clement Vaulkhurst, and now I—of all people—have the chance to work closely with him and to have his help in writing the thesis? He's chased away anyone else who ever tried to penetrate the wall of privacy he's built around himself."

Hughbank scowled. He began pacing around the room, losing a bit of his cool self-control. "I can understand why he doesn't want anyone writing about his private life! It's not very respectable, from what I've heard."

"You've heard what everybody else has heard. And that's why I want to write the truth about him. Because most of what you've 'heard' isn't true at all. I've seen him at work. He's a dedicated and sensitive artist. Sure, he's a bit unconventional. But the stories about his enormous drinking bouts and the women who flock around him are exaggerated. Why, if you listened to the gossips, you'd think he's running a harem."

Bill glared at her. "Now you're defending him!"

"I am not!" she said hotly—and was somewhat disconcerted when she realized how impulsively she had leaped to Clement's defense. "I'm—I'm just trying to be truthful. There are a lot of things I don't like about him. He's egocentric, vain, temperamental, and dictatorial. But he's not exactly the Casanova the gossip magazines make him out to be. As a matter of fact, I only know of one woman he's involved with, an artist who has been close to him for quite some time."

Bill shook his head. "All of that might very well be true. But it doesn't alter the fact that you are living

under his roof. Deborah, I have the utmost respect for
you, and I want to trust you and believe you. But
you've put a pretty big strain on my faith in you. I have
to admit that I'm pretty confused about this situation
and your behavior. This just isn't like you at all. You're
behaving like a stranger."

"Well—"

"If you didn't have any consideration for my feelings,
have you thought about your parents and their position
at the university? A scandal involving their daughter
would not be good for their careers."

Deborah was feeling more miserable by the minute.
She was aware of all her old inhibitions taking hold
again. The brave new world she had fashioned for
herself was coming apart at the seams. Bill was getting
her confused and flustered. Her thinking was becoming
muddled.

It was true that she had acted impulsively and
selfishly. She hadn't given any thought to Bill or to her
family when she'd accepted Clement's proposal to help
her with her thesis if she would move into his home and
work with him this summer. She had only thought of
the wonderful opportunity it presented. Now she was
beginning to feel like a traitor to Bill and to her family.
"I'm—I'm sorry," she said through stiff lips.

Deborah spent the next two hours talking with Bill
Hughbank. They argued, going over the same ground
repeatedly, and after two hours nothing was resolved.
Deborah was miserable and emotionally exhausted.
Bill had succeeded in loading her down with guilt. But,
torn as she was by the painful battle going on inside
herself between the old, conventional, inhibited girl she
had been and the new, independent woman she had
become, Deborah clung stubbornly to one resolve: she

was not going to give up this once-in-a-lifetime opportunity to achieve something important.

"You're just going to have to trust me, Bill," Deborah said.

They parted on cool terms, Bill looking forlorn and baffled, and Deborah still feeling like a traitor.

Clement was not at the mansion that night when she returned to her room, and he did not put in an appearance for the next two days. Deborah assumed he had gone off somewhere with Serna. She went on with her daily routine of typing his edited manuscript. Bill was staying at Doug Carpenter's motel. He'd given no indication about when he might leave. Deborah suspected he was going to stick around to keep an eye on her. She had mixed feelings about the situation. Bill had been an important part of her life for some time, and he represented a certain predictable security that she found reassuring. They had similar backgrounds and were comfortable together, as long as she did not have to question her emotions about him.

Each afternoon when she finished her typing for the day, she drove into town and had dinner with Bill at one of the local restaurants. Deborah was aware of the curious stares and knew she was giving the town gossips more juicy material to speculate about. But she was not concerned about them. She had other, more important problems of her own on her mind.

On the third day Clement returned, looking somewhat the worse for wear. He pulled into the driveway at ten thirty in the morning and came stomping into the house. They were having one of the torrential rains that periodically descended on the marshy east Texas pine forests. Clement stood in the doorway of the study, dripping water and scowling at Deborah. He needed a shave, and his eyes were bloodshot. "Must you make such an infernal racket with that typewriter?"

She met his gaze cooly, rolling a fresh sheet of paper into the machine. "I gather that you are hung over."

"I'm not hung over. I have a tension headache."

She shrugged. "Call it what you wish. How is Serna? Does she have a 'tension headache,' too?"

"What is that supposed to mean?"

"Well, it's apparent you've been off somewhere carousing with her the past two days."

He gave her a malevolent grin. "Does that disturb you?"

She shrugged. "It's absolutely no concern of mine." But inwardly she felt angry and wasn't sure why.

"Why do you automatically assume that Serna and I have been together the last two days?"

"It's obvious, isn't it? Look, your personal life is your own business. I have to get back to my typing. I want to finish this chapter today."

He came around to her side, picking up some of the pages she had typed, and read them quickly. "Your typing is as neat and precise as you are."

She was feeling more angry by the minute. Why did he always do this to her? He was standing close to her, and that was somehow disturbing and added fuel to her anger.

He put the page down and looked at her in a way that made her uncomfortable. "I hear your boyfriend is in town."

She frowned. "Do you have spies out checking on me?"

An infuriating smile tugged at his lips. "Hardly. As you know, this town has an active gossip grapevine. I stopped at Harry's Diner on the way into town this morning for a cup of coffee and to catch up on the local news. I was given a detailed account of your romantic activities since I've been gone, how you've been mooning over your young Lothario at dinner in the local cafés every evening."

She flushed angrily. "Yes, Bill flew down to see me, and we have had dinner together. I don't call it 'mooning.'"

He merely chuckled. "What is he, a grammar-school physical-education teacher?"

"A lawyer."

"Oh, a *lawyer.*"

"Bill is a fine, dependable, and considerate person," she said, and added in her private thoughts, Which is more than I can say for you, Clement Vaulkhurst!

"He sounds terribly dull."

"I don't find him so," she retorted, raising her chin defiantly. She had forgotten how maddening Clement Vaulkhurst could be. The more Clement irritated and baited her, the more attractive Bill became.

"Well," he said, "I must get out of these wet clothes." He started out of the room, then paused in the doorway. "By the way, I have not spent the past two days with Serna. Sorry to disappoint your overactive imagination. The fact is, I've been in Houston, battling over contract details with my agent, who flew there from the West Coast. I'm giving a dinner party tomorrow night. My agent will be here. There will also be a Hollywood producer who wants to discuss film rights on one of my novels. Serna will act as hostess.

You may invite your lawyer boyfriend. Perhaps he can add something to the conversation, though I doubt it."

The dinner was preceded by cocktails, served in the spacious living room of the mansion. A white-jacketed bartender kept the guests supplied with beverages. Deborah had half expected Clement to have Indian Red provide fried catfish for the dinner, but a local caterer had been hired for the event. Serna had seen to it that the dinner had a more civilized character.

Deborah felt totally outclassed when the glamorous Hungarian artist made her entrance. Serna wore a breathtaking white cocktail gown that paid a seductive compliment to her exquisite figure. The gown made use of the narrow shoulder-strap style of the twenties combined with a revealing contemporary slit up both sides of the clinging skirt to entice the male eye. The bodice was low cut in a deep V, exposing a swell of breast obviously not hampered by a bra. The back was cut low, leaving bare flesh as smooth as the silky texture of the dress. The skirt clung artfully to her rounded hips. Whenever the artist moved, the slitted skirt gave flashing peeks of her shapely legs.

Serna gave Deborah a triumphant and scathing look, dismissing her prim, sexless gown as a total washout, and devoted her entire attention to Clement and the other men for the remainder of the evening.

Deborah felt like a clod in the light-blue chiffon and taffeta evening dress she had worn to several faculty parties back home. Hugging her throat was a thin band of blue taffeta edged with matching blue lace, in the center of which clustered a dainty blue bow. The bodice and long, full sleeves were lined with the same blue taffeta, as was the floor-length skirt. The covering chiffon was shirred in the front, and the skirt was gathered at the tight waistband.

I'm not showing an inch of bare skin. I look as formless as a sack with a string drawn round the middle, she thought grimly, eyeing the self-assured, seductively attired artist with sullen envy. Beside the older, sophisticated woman, Deborah felt every bit the conventional, spinsterish schoolgirl that Clement had accused her of being.

After torturing herself with a lengthy appraisal of the other female, Deborah swung her attention to the men in the room.

Clement dominated the group with his dark, powerful physique. He towered over the agent and the Hollywood producer. His personality was an electrifying force, making the air in the room crackle. A white dinner jacket hugged his broad shoulders.

Bill was as tall as Clement, but built along more slender, lithe lines. The two men contrasted in every respect, Bill's fair, light hair directly opposed to Clement's shock of unruly black thatch. Bill looked cool and well tailored in his white dinner jacket. His manner was reserved, carefully controlled. Clement, on the other hand, gave the impression of a force field.

Clement's literary agent, Eli McIntire, was a man of medium height with gray hair and a chronically nervous, worried expression. The Hollywood producer, Ron Glasser, was the only man not wearing a dinner jacket. Instead, he sported a shirt casually unbuttoned nearly to the waist. A heavy gold pendant dangled against his deeply tanned chest. Balding and slightly overweight, he gave Deborah the impression of a middle-aged man trying desperately to look half his age.

Clement's agent got Deborah aside. "Clement tells me you are a relative."

She nodded. "A distant cousin."

"He said you're helping type the final draft of his new novel."

"Yes. We'll be through next week, I think. Then he's going to help me write a biographical thesis about his life."

"Most unusual for Clement to allow anyone to get so close to his work. He's rather paranoid about that. He must think very highly of you."

"Well, let's just say he seems to trust me."

The agent gulped his highball, put his glass down, and nervously lit a cigarette. "Perhaps you can help me, Miss Denhoff."

"Help you?" she asked with surprise.

"Yes, with Clement. This movie deal could mean a great deal of money for him—for us. But I'm afraid of what will happen if he starts talking with Ron."

"What do you mean?"

Eli McIntire sighed. "You know Clement. He doesn't care what he says to anybody. He once insulted the governor of the state. Some kind of literary-award affair. The governor made a stupid remark about a piece of literature. Clement suggested that he should stick to what he knew something about—raising hogs on his farm in west Texas."

A smile tugged at Deborah's lips. "That sounds like Clement, all right."

"Exactly. You can see why I'm worried. Let's face it: Ron is something of a phony. He's into all the typical

California pop/chic/psycho affectations: mind expansion, est, transcendental meditation, astrology, hot tubs—you name it, and he's in it; he's absorbed all the cliché phrases. The guy is not overly bright, and Clement is going to have a field day with him. I'm praying that Ron will be too stupid to realize Clement is insulting him. I was hoping—since you seem to have an inside track with Clement—that you might persuade him to go easy on Ron. If the guy goes back to California in a huff, we can kiss a quarter of a million in movie rights goodbye."

Deborah sighed and shook her head. "I don't have any 'inside track' with Clement, Mr. McIntire. And I certainly don't have any control over him. As far as he's concerned, I'm merely part of the furniture around here—an extension of his electric typewriter."

The agent looked harassed and defeated. "I have a bleeding ulcer. You want to know why? Because Clement gave it to me. That's why." He swallowed a pill and walked off.

At the dinner table, Serna sat at Clement's right hand and acted toward him in a possessive manner. She was making it clear to the guests that she held a place of special importance in the household. Deborah sat next to Bill, who wore an expression of aloofness and disapproval every time he glanced in Clement's direction.

As the dinner progressed, Deborah was uncomfortably aware of the undercurrent of antagonism between Clement and Bill. She was quite aware that having Deborah and her "square" boyfriend present appealed to Clement's cutting sense of humor. He was scornful of Bill's rigid, knee-jerk conventionality. Bill, on the other hand, considered Vaulkhurst to be a maverick, a bohemian, a renegade, and a threat to his idea of an orderly, controlled, predictable society.

Across the table from Deborah, Eli McIntire shot nervous glances from Clement to Ron Glasser and wiped his perspiring palms on his napkin every time Clement directed a remark to the Hollywood producer.

"Clement," Ron Glasser said at one point, "I want you to know that I'm absolutely into your writing and what it says. You're into the essence of your people, especially in *Return to Evil*. I got deeply into the protagonist . . . a man who had to have his own space. I can dig that."

Clement stared at him with one eyebrow raised. "Oh, then you do actually read books."

Glasser looked at him blankly. "Oh, yes. Santayana, the Maharishi, Erhard's est. I really dig Werner Erhard."

"Do you really, now? You actually dig him, do you?"

Across from Deborah, Eli McIntire swallowed another pill and wiped his perspiring brow. He was making eye signals to Clement, who ignored him.

Ron Glasser plowed on. "Yes, I can see the symbolism in *Return to Evil*. Very heavy stuff. Very heavy, man. I see it as the protagonist at last becoming resigned to his karma."

"Oh, indeed?" Clement pursed his lips. "I'm so glad you told me, Mr. Glasser. You know, it's really amazing the way your brain works. I've never run into another quite like it."

Glasser beamed, too dense to understand the sarcasm in Clement's words.

Eli McIntire looked appealingly at Deborah, but she could only give a faint shrug while she stifled a grin. By now she knew Clement well enough to realize that nothing was going to stop him from dismantling the pompous producer. She could see he was warming up to the situation like a hunter setting his prey up for the kill.

"Tell me more about my protagonist's karma, Mr. Glasser. You have me fascinated."

At that point, Serna interrupted Clement's cat-and-mouse game. "Let's have coffee on the veranda. It's lovely out there this time of the evening."

Ron Glasser looked disappointed, while Eli McIntire appeared enormously relieved.

The group adjourned to the flagstone veranda which overlooked the garden and swimming pool. Ron Glasser tried to get Clement cornered to continue their conversation, but Serna slipped her arm through Clement's and pouted, "Please take me for a walk, darling. I'm absolutely stifled after that meal."

Serna led Clement down around the pool and past a row of hedges. McIntire and the film producer began talking contracts. Deborah and Bill strolled to the edge of the veranda.

The night air felt heavy from the surrounding dense vegetation of the marshy, semitropical jungle. Deborah could hear the call of night birds off in the Big Thicket. A shiver ran through her. "It's beautiful, and yet a little frightening. I'd hate to be lost out there in the Thicket this time of night. Do you know there are alligators, bears, and even a nearly extinct kind of panther roaming that jungle?"

"Not a very pretty place," Bill muttered.

"It depends. To city folks like us it seems wild and primitive and dangerous. But exquisite flowers grow there, wild orchids for example, and birds you won't find anywhere else. To a nature lover, a bird watcher, a botanist, it's one of the few last unspoiled natural paradises."

"Well, I'll be happy when you get this out of your system and are ready to return to a more civilized life," Bill said.

"You still think this is all just a silly whim of mine, don't you?" she challenged.

"I don't know, Deborah. Frankly, I can't see a lot of value in it."

"A biography of Clement Vaulkhurst will be of enormous value to the literary world."

"I suppose"—he sighed—"though, frankly, I don't have much use for the man."

She restrained a smile. "I sensed that he has about the same opinion of you."

"Well, he's welcome to his opinion. I can't see what you find so fascinating about him. He's rude and egotistical."

"He's rude only in terms of the polite, superficial, phony surface manners we exhibit. He has a way of dismissing sham that can be disconcerting. As for being egotistical, he is that, I suppose, but it's because he's conscious of his own genius and impatient with lesser minds—"

She suddenly broke off her little lecture, realizing that she was again defending Clement. Why, she wondered, did she instinctively defend him to Bill, when most of the time she was saying the very things to herself that Bill had just said about him? She felt baffled by her own behavior and decided that the safest course was to change the subject.

"Come on," she said, tugging at Bill's arm. "Let's walk down by the pool."

They walked in silence, each lost in thought. Debo-

rah had fallen under the spell of the night and the
mysterious jungle swamp so close to them. She felt out
of touch with her own twentieth-century world. The
distant, plaintive night call of an exotic bird in the Big
Thicket caught at her throat and sent a shiver down her
spine. It was like the lost cry of a nameless creature in
the steaming swamp of a prehistoric age.

They wandered past the swimming pool and into the
garden with its rows of neatly trimmed hedges. Moonlight bathed the garden with a silvery patina. Deborah
heard the crunch of gravel under their feet. This section
of the garden was terraced. When they walked around a
bend in the hedge, a lower level of the garden became
visible. Deborah suddenly paused, immobilized by a
scene at the perimeter of her vision. She glanced up at
Bill, but he was looking in another direction. She let
her gaze swim back and focus for a painful second.

There below, half screened by trees and hedges but
spotlighted by a patch of silvery moonlight, stood two
figures locked in embrace—Clement and Serna.

Deborah became aware of a thundering pulse in her
head, a tight fist squeezing her heart. A portion of her
rational mind thought calmly, So what? It was no
concern of hers. She already knew Serna was Clement's
paramour, didn't she? What would be more natural
than for him to kiss her in this romantic setting? Why
should it matter to Deborah? But for some irrational
reason it did—very much. Her emotions weren't calm
at all. A feeling very basic and very female was boiling
inside her. Perhaps it was actually seeing them in each
other's arms. . . . She couldn't explain it—didn't try.
At the moment she was in no mood for self-analysis.
Whatever the reason for the irrational emotions storm-
ing inside her, they took hold and controlled her.

She held Bill's arm tighter and steered him away, back up the path. She didn't know why, but she did not want Bill to see what she had just witnessed. Somehow she considered it a private matter between Serna, Clement, and herself.

Bill was saying something about the lush growth in the garden. She answered distractedly. Then she heard footsteps coming up the path from below, crunching the gravel softly.

"Bill," she blurted out impulsively, "kiss me."

He blinked at her. "What?"

"Well, do you want to kiss me or not?"

He grinned. "Sure." And he promptly obliged her.

She was in his arms, returning his kiss with an ardor that surprised them both, when the footsteps came closer.

At last she stepped back, somewhat breathlessly, and moments later Clement and Serna moved past them. They had obviously seen the kiss. Deborah caught a glimpse of Clement's face. He wore an expression of dark displeasure.

For some reason, she felt a kind of perverse triumph.

Chapter Eight

Deborah was at her desk in the study bright and early the next morning. Clement put in an appearance shortly after she'd rolled her first sheet of paper in the typewriter. "Good morning," she said coolly.

He grunted a sour reply.

She began typing, trying to ignore him.

Clement prowled around the room, picking up books and closing them, shuffling papers. Finally he slumped in a chair and scowled at her.

She became aware of his dark, brooding stare fixed on her. She began making more than her usual number of typing errors. "I wish you'd stop staring at me," she finally said in exasperation. "You're making me nervous."

"Where is your boyfriend, the adolescent lawyer?"

She glared at him. "I'd hardly call Bill an adolescent. He's twenty-five, a college graduate, and ready to take his bar examination."

"Twenty-five," Vaulkhurst said scornfully. "When does he apply for Medicare?"

"My, you're in a fine mood this morning."

His only reply was a deepening scowl.

"As for where Bill is, he went back to his motel early last night after the dinner. I can't say you did much to make him feel welcome here. You were barely civil to him."

"Did you go with him?"

"Where?"

"To his motel, of course. Don't be so dense."

She gave him a cool stare. "Why," she asked, "would a conventional, spinsterish type like me—according to your own description—do anything as wicked as that?"

His eyes were smoldering with dark embers. "After that disgusting display of your childish necking with him in the garden, I may revise my evaluation of your virginity."

An angry flush spread over her cheeks. "That innocent kiss," she retorted, "could hardly compare with the vulgar display that took place between you and Serna."

He raised an eyebrow. "So you were spying on us?"

"I'd hardly go to that effort," she flung back at him. "We just happened to stroll past a gap in the hedge and there you were. You could at least confine such lewd behavior to a more discreet place."

He gave her a chilling look. "Perhaps it was as innocent as you claim your embrace with Hughbank was."

"Oh, I'll believe *that* when the Sahara desert turns into a rain forest!"

Vaulkhurst arose and towered over her. She could see, just past his shoulder, the portrait Serna had painted of him. His face in real life was a mirrored reflection of the brooding inner rages captured so powerfully in the portrait. "I'd like to know one thing," he continued. "Exactly what do you see in that pallid, insipid, unimaginative pipsqueak?"

She stood up, her knees trembling with anger. "How dare you use that kind of language about Bill?"

"I dare because it's the truth," he raged. "If you haven't sense enough to see it for yourself, perhaps I should enlighten you."

"I don't recall that I asked your opinion," she retorted, anger pumping adrenaline through her veins, making her heart pound and her breathing grow rapid.

"Nevertheless, I'm giving it to you. And one day you'll thank me. I've come to know you quite well, Deborah. In spite of some of your childish inhibitions, you do have considerable depth of character—a surprising degree of sensitivity and imagination. That man will stifle all individuality out of you. He'll turn you into a plastic robot, who repeats all the platitudes of his phony, artificial world."

Then Deborah did something that horrified and stunned her . . . something that she did not plan and seemed unable to control. Blinding tears had half obscured Clement's face. His words were like daggers, stabbing some deep, private place of hurting conflict within her. She reacted like a wounded animal striking out at a tormentor who had her cornered and was stripping her of all her defenses.

She slapped Clement with a ringing blow that stung her palm and left a red print on his cheek.

There was an instant of shocked silence. She caught her breath and held it, her teeth clamped on her bottom lip, her eyes wide with horror. Clement looked like a frozen charge of high explosive. She could almost hear his fuse blazing up to the charge that was going to blow up in her face in the next few seconds. Her panicked mind told her that this dark, threatening man was capable of anything, and she had pushed him too far.

Suddenly, his powerful hands dragged her from behind her desk. He pulled her into a crushing embrace. Then he kissed her angrily, brutally, in a way she had never before been kissed. His mouth was cruelly demanding. At first she was frozen with fright and rebellion. And then a fire ignited deep within her. All her nerve ends awoke with an electrifying charge. Her body quivered with a thundering passion beyond anything she had ever before known. Gasping, half out of her mind with desire, she welcomed the bruising power of his embrace, his kiss. His cruelty was fuel that fed the fire raging out of control within her. Her heart beat in rhythm with his. Her body was molded to his powerful male contours. She met the strength of his embrace with her own strength.

In her swirling senses, the dimensions of time and space evaporated. There was only this kiss, this avalanche of emotions in an eternity privately their own . . . a moment that encompassed all feeling, all experiences, from the earliest mists of creation to the final disintegration of the universe.

At last his kiss ended. She sagged in his arms, breathless, her legs barely able to support her. Clement's eyes, black as anthracite and deep with a knowledge of life far beyond her young years, searched hers, taking possession of her soul as his embrace had possessed her emotions and body.

Finally he said, "So much for that boyfriend of

yours. That kiss should prove to you beyond a doubt that he's not for you. Don't try to tell me you ever responded to one of his kisses like that."

Deborah shuddered, gathering her strength and pulling away from him. Tears trickled down her cheeks. She turned away from him, hot with shame now. "Why do you do things like that to me?"

"For your own good. You don't know your own mind."

"And I suppose you do!"

"Better than you, little one."

"It's my life! Let me live it my way."

"Let you ruin it your way, you mean. You don't love Bill Hughbank. How could you love him and kiss another man the way you just responded to me? Do you plan to throw your life away on him?"

She faced him, seeing his face through her streaming tears. "Stop meddling in my life! I may not be wild with passion with Bill, but he can offer me a great deal— much that is important to a woman . . . to me. Marriage, for one thing. Respect. Decency. Steadfastness. A home and children. A solid life of self-respect and security. I'm very fond of him now, I'm quite sure of that, and I'll grow to love him more. He's going to be the father of my children."

Their eyes clashed in mortal combat. Vaulkhurst looked both scornful and perplexed. At last, he threw his hands up. "Stubborn, stubborn, stubborn! Very well; go stifle yourself in your conventional little existence. I don't know why I waste my time with you."

He slammed out of the room.

Shaken and distraught, Deborah gave up trying to do any more work that morning. She went to her room, where she paced back and forth, alternating between anger and tears. She hated herself for allowing Clement to get her so upset. Why couldn't she simply ignore him? Time and again she had told herself that the best way to cope with a man like him was to not allow him to get under her skin.

Then she remembered her first introduction to Clement Vaulkhurst, when she had seen his portrait in his study that night she had ventured into the house. And she remembered in vivid detail the unexpected flood of emotions that the striking portrait had awakened in her. Just seeing his portrait had done that to her! Then, later, she had met the man himself, and the emotions had become stormier, more convulsing.

No, she admitted, Clement Vaulkhurst was not a man that a woman could ignore. Hate him, yes. Despise him, yes. Be fascinated by him, certainly—and at the same time infuriated by him. He did all of those things to her, and there was no way she could simply turn off her feelings and become cool and objective about the man. And that, in itself, was maddening.

She recalled her parents' warning about this summer trip and about her plans to come in contact with the notorious writer. Now she realized more clearly why they had objected. They had known the danger she was walking into and had tried to warn her, to shield her from exactly the kind of emotional turmoil she was going through now. She had plunged ahead recklessly, eager for her first taste of adventure, of freedom, wanting to drink more deeply of life with all its highs and lows. Well, she'd done exactly that, and right at the moment she felt cowardly. She wished she were back in her safe, familiar room in her family's home on the campus, in her bed, with the covers pulled over her head.

She had prowled restlessly around her room for an hour, resolving none of the conflicts that stormed through her heart, but at least growing calmer and more in command of herself, when there was a tap at her door. Then a woman's voice.

It was Serna Czerny. "May I talk with you?" the artist asked in a cool, formal manner, a tone that made it clear they remained enemies.

"I—I don't feel like talking right now. Could we make it later?" Deborah replied through the door.

"No, I have to talk to you now. We're driving into Houston this morning to take Eli and Ron Glasser back to the airport. Clement wants you to go with us."

Deborah opened the door. She faced Serna, who was her usual cool, self-possessed person, glamorous and smartly dressed even this early in the morning.

"Why does he want me to go?" Deborah asked.

Serna shrugged. "I suppose to help keep Ron entertained. The more people there are in the car, the less apt Clement is to antagonize him. As you could see at dinner last night, Clement can't stand the man. He's a complete and utter phony—exactly the type that sets Clement off. So far, Eli has been able to keep them separated. Eli wants you and him in the back seat with Ron. I'll sit in the front with Clement. With a bit of luck, Eli hopes they can get Ron safely on the plane before Clement totally destroys the chance for this film contract. A few more exchanges between Clement and Ron and it's finally going to dawn on the producer that Clement is making an ass out of him."

Deborah thought of the two-hour drive into Houston in the same car with Clement. She wasn't sure if her nerves could stand it. "I'd really rather not go."

Serna shrugged. "Clement said to tell you that this was included in your duties since you were working for him this summer. As for myself, I think the trip would be more pleasant if you weren't along."

More pleasant if you had Clement all to yourself, is what you mean, Deborah thought with an unexpected flash of anger.

"Well . . . let me think about it for a few minutes," Deborah hedged.

"Don't take all morning making up your mind. We're leaving in fifteen minutes."

Serna left. Deborah stood in the same spot, besieged by a new battle of emotions. She knew, even before Serna walked away, that she was going to go to Houston with them. Why, she wasn't sure. Something about the possessive manner in which Serna had said she was riding in the front seat with Clement had irked Deborah. The reason for that wasn't clear to her, either. However, she rationalized that she was working for Clement in a manner of speaking, and he had relayed the message that this was part of her duties. So she would go. Perhaps she'd have the opportunity to do some shopping while in Houston. That would be a welcome distraction from tension that had been tearing her apart.

The ride into Houston was anything but relaxing. Below the casual surface conversations there were ebb tides of tension. Eli McIntire was a nervous wreck, trying to keep Clement and the producer from getting into an exchange that would offend Glasser. Deborah was doing a slow burn at the way Serna was snuggling up to Clement in the front seat. Even more infuriating was the fact that he didn't object at all and even appeared to enjoy it. Once she caught his eye in the rearview mirror, glancing at her, and saw an amused smirk on his lips that gave her a wrench of fury.

When they entered the freeway exchange into Houston, Clement told them that he had several business matters to take care of after they left the airport. It would be dark before they returned to Uromund. Serna elected to spend the afternoon at her hairdresser's. Deborah expressed a desire to go shopping at one of Houston's glamorous malls.

They saw the agent and producer safely off at the airport. Then Clement drove to the mall Deborah had chosen. She stood beside the mall entrance, watching Clement's Mercedes pull away into the stream of traffic, Serna still glued close to his side.

"That *woman!*" Deborah exploded.

Then she determined she would put Serna and Clement completely out of her mind. She would find escape in a shopping spree. In her purse were a comfortable number of traveler's checks that she had brought from home to finance her summer. She was suddenly in a mood to indulge herself recklessly—like a person about to step into a bar and go on a weekend binge.

She strolled down the air-conditioned mall, looking into the windows of shops and boutiques. She was surrounded by a constantly moving stream of humanity: well-dressed people hurrying past, couples ambling hand in hand, children standing in front of a small wishing-well pond, where pennies gleamed on the blue tile bottom. Elderly men and women sat on concrete benches, some dozing, others looking with interest at the moving shoppers. A music system provided a soft background of melody just audible above the bustle of the busy mall. There were indoor gardens, waterfalls, escalators rising to the second level.

The interior of a shopping mall was a microcosm of the larger world outside, Deborah thought. She sensed an electric charge in the air, as if something important were about to happen, and she wondered vaguely where she fit into all this teeming life around her. She had a strange feeling of detachment from the Deborah Denhoff who had left the university campus only a few weeks ago to research her famous cousin Clement Vaulkhurst. She was being swept along on a rising level of excitement by the busy atmosphere of the mall.

It was a strange sensation. All the people in this mammoth structure were, in a sense, sharing their lives for a moment as they conducted their day's activities shielded from the heat, pollution, and traffic noises of one of the richest, fastest-growing cities in the world, sprawling just outside. It was as if they had made a secret pact with one another when they entered here to become temporary citizens of the mall, a city, a world, in itself, and that pact terminated when they left the security of the mall.

Deborah noticed a young woman sitting on one of the mall benches. The girl had very pretty features, but she did nothing to enhance her looks. Her blond hair wasn't attractively styled. Her clothes were plain and dowdy, hiding rather than flattering her figure. On her feet were practical but ugly flat shoes.

Then Deborah glanced toward a mirror in one of the shop windows, and she saw a counterpart of the girl on the bench—herself! The same tasteless dress, an equal-

ly unflattering hair style . . . a total downplaying of figure and features that could make her attractive with
the proper styling.

Clement's appraisal of her suddenly echoed in her
ears: ". . . spinsterish . . . tasteless clothes. . . ."

She had promised herself that she was not going to
allow thoughts of Clement Vaulkhurst to spoil her
shopping trips, but he intruded on her thoughts now,
because in a flash she saw herself from his viewpoint.

Instantly, she became furious. Just when she was
getting a taste of independence and freedom, he had
undermined her self-confidence by pointing out how
frumpy she looked. If he was such a great writer and
had so much insight into human nature, couldn't he see
how tenuous was the grip she had on her new independence?

Suddenly a new, shocking thought assailed her. Was
it possible that Clement planned to make her one of the
characters in his next novel—a conventional, hidebound square, as he called her—and had continually
baited her to test her reactions? Knowing how ruthless
he was, she thought it entirely possible. He cared little
about people as human beings. They were material for
his creative laboratory.

She became filled with rage toward him all over
again. With the anger came a surge of resentment and
rebellion. Perhaps she'd just show him an entirely
different Deborah Denhoff. How exquisite it would be
to see the shock on his face. And she'd enjoy turning
the tables on Serna Czerny, too. That woman—
Deborah always referred to her in her mind as *that
woman*—invariably looked at Deborah as if she were a
provincial clod who barely knew how to comb her hair.

Deborah glanced at her watch. Just enough time this

afternoon to carry out the sudden daring plan that had
blazed up in her mind. She located a display board with
the mall directory, ran her finger down the list of shops
until she located two likely-looking places on the upper
level, and then took the escalator. She found the
beauty shop. *No Appointment Necessary,* proclaimed a
sign in the window. She took a deep breath, screwed up
her courage, and walked in.

Two hours later, Deborah emerged from the shop,
her head reeling from shock. She was stunned that
she'd had the nerve to approach the shopowner, a tall,
gray-haired woman with an artificial smile, and ask for
a complete new styling from hair to makeup.

"I want you to make me as beautiful as possible,"
Deborah had said recklessly. "Just do whatever you
think best. But I'm in a hurry."

A gleam had sparkled in the woman's eyes. Probably, Deborah had thought, most patrons came into her
shop with fixed ideas about how they should look.
Deborah was placing herself totally in the beautician's
hands, and she viewed it as a professional challenge
. . . one in which she had carte blanche.

Her hair had been styled with a layered look that
required only a few minutes to cut. Then it was blown
dry. Finally, the beautician touched on a hint of rouge
and gave Deborah a running commentary on how to
apply her makeup to re-create her new look whenever
she chose. Then Deborah's chair was swung around so
she faced a large mirror.

She gasped. Her dark hair looked fuller than she had
ever seen it—the result of a professional cut. Her large
green eyes looked luminous and had taken on swirling
depths beneath the long lashes. For the first time, she
realized that the pixie face she'd been born with had

great possibilities. Her nose was delicate and well shaped, and her lips looked full and sensual with the frosted lipstick that had been chosen for her. She looked . . . glamorous. She could find no other word to describe her new appearance. There was an aliveness about her face that had been missing before. She wasn't sure whether it was due entirely to the makeup and hair styling; maybe it was due in part to an inner glow she felt at seeing herself look so ravishing. Now she knew the glamorous features had been there all along; it had taken professional knowledge and the right application of cosmetics to bring them out.

The next thing Deborah knew, she was standing out in the mall traffic again, clutching a parcel filled with cosmetics, and her head was swimming as she realized how much money she had just parted with in order to achieve her new look.

But as she passed a mirror-veneered post, she was so struck by her new appearance that she thought the expense had been well worth every cent it had cost her. Why had she never before thought that she deserved to spend her own money on making herself look more attractive? Was it because her family placed so much emphasis on intellectual achievement, and she had wanted so desperately to meet their standards in that area, that she had purposely or unconsciously neglected her physical attributes?

Deborah smiled approvingly at her image as she studied her face. But then she saw that her facial transformation made her clothes look even more dowdy. Everything from the plain, round collar of her dress to her practical wedge heels was all wrong. She definitely needed a new outfit to complete her transformation. She wondered what her grandfather would think of how she was spending her inheritance money. But when she considered the exhilarating boost to her morale this shopping trip was giving her, she thought he would surely approve. After all, she was on the verge of finding out who and what she was. What better use could she make of the small inheritance left her by her grandfather?

It was with a new, confident stride that Deborah moved down the mall, in search of the kind of shop that would satisfy her wardrobe needs. She felt an overwhelming desire to splurge on herself, and she wanted to locate a store before the mood escaped her.

She rounded a corner, and there, in a shopwindow, looking as if the designer had fashioned it only for her, was a deep purple dress that set Deborah's heart pounding. It had a rounded neckline banded by a thin sequined braid that coordinated with the spaghetti shoulder straps. The stretch lace material was form fitting. It covered a lining the color of bare skin. The skirt was slit daringly up the front so a flash of leg showed with every movement of the wearer. Deborah suppressed a naughty giggle, but she knew it was the dress she must own. Without a moment's hesitation, she entered the shop, pointed to the dress on the mannequin, and in moments found herself in the dressing room, staring at the reflection of a lovely young woman she hardly knew but was beginning to like. Miraculously, the dress required no alterations; she suspected it had been made for her, hugging her tightly around her small waist and curving provocatively to her compact hips.

Deborah blushed, seeing how much of her figure was revealed by the curves of the dress. But her new, daring mood gave her the courage to wear it.

A saleslady entered the dressing room. "Perfect!" she exclaimed. "Just perfect on you. Are you a model, my dear? You certainly are lovely!"

"No," Deborah replied, "but thank you. That's certainly good for my ego."

"Well, you should be a model. If you wore that dress at a style show, we'd sell out in record time."

Deborah felt her self-confidence climbing rapidly. Maybe, she thought, the dress wasn't too daring after all. Perhaps she was too much aware of how the dress showed off her figure only because she had hidden for so long under plain, shapeless garments that did absolutely nothing for her.

"I'll take it," Deborah said impulsively, then gnawed at her bottom lip and stared wide-eyed at her reflection in the mirror as if saying, Well, Deborah Denhoff, now you've done it!

"What else do you have?" Deborah asked as the saleslady helped with the dress zipper.

For the next hour, Deborah tried on an assortment of sports wear, street dresses, and evening wear. Every outfit looked stunning on her, and she realized for the first time how much a combination of professional makeup, a good hair style, and smartly designed clothes could contribute to the overall aura of glamor exuded so well by Serna Czerny.

While Deborah was different from Serna in every conceivable way, she knew she was equally glamorous. She was on even terms with the older woman now, at least in the looks department. She wondered briefly how Serna would react to Deborah's new image, but that question was immediately superseded by a more important one: How would Clement react?

While part of her was bent on improving her appearance simply because she no longer fit into the old mold, another part of her, she knew, was reacting to Clement's challenge to her femininity, and she began to realize with an undercurrent of anxiety that Clement's reaction to her was somehow extremely important. He had given her the incentive to change, had goaded and badgered her until she had to react—and now his response would be a reflection of the success of her transformation. While her new look was merely an outer change, it symbolized an important inner change in her feelings about how she looked at herself.

It wasn't until Deborah was leaving the store with a large assortment of bags filled with an array of garments and several pairs of shoes unlike any she had ever worn before in her life that she gave any thought to Bill Hughbank. And her parents. They would be surprised, perhaps a bit shocked, but her parents she could cope with. She wasn't so sure about Bill. He had some pretty staid, conventional, and fixed ideas about how she should look and act. Was she really strong enough at this point to handle him? Would she waffle under his objections about her radical change in appearance and his questions about her motives, and meekly slink back into her old mold and hide in the safety of the tired old clothes that had protected her so long?

Yes, now she realized why she had shied away from glamorous hair styles and makeup and had chosen formless, practical garments. She had been afraid to be herself, to pick out the kinds of clothes that gave her a zing, that made her feel feminine and alluring. She had wanted to feel safe, to prove to her parents, to Bill, to the family and university milieu, that, like her brother

and sister, intellectual achievement was all-important.
She had been afraid of anything that might appear
frivolous and call attention to herself. To sum it up
quite neatly, she had simply been afraid to be herself.

But how could she be herself when she hadn't known
who she really was? Now she was finding out, and it was
an exciting experience. For the first time in her confined
existence, she felt like taking chances and tasting life.
New challenges lay ahead. She had found in herself the
grit to tackle them head on, come what may.

Deborah whisked down the mall concourse, her
shoulders held back, her breasts straining at the red
knit top that hugged her curves tightly. A red and black
skirt snapped about her legs, calling attention to the
smooth curve of her calves and the trim line of her
ankles.

She was waiting outside the mall entrance at the
appointed time. With her pulse quickening, she
watched the cars moving past, searching for a familiar
Mercedes. At last it came into view, turned down one
of the thoroughfare lanes, and pulled up at the
entrance.

Clement was alone in the car. He looked at her
blankly as she moved down from the sidewalk and
approached the car. Balancing her load of parcels in
one arm, she negotiated the rear door latch. She
deposited the boxes on the rear seat. Then she opened
the front door and slid in beside Clement.

He was still staring at her. She adjusted her seat belt,
crossed her legs, and smiled at him. "Where's Serna?"

She was somehow managing a calm exterior, but
inwardly she was all aflutter. What was Clement
thinking? What would he say? She tried to read the
expression in his eyes but could not. She could not

recall ever before in her life being so painfully self-conscious.

She was on the verge of panic, wondering if she'd done the right thing. She had thought the new hair style, makeup, and clothes made her look attractive. But what if she was wrong? What if they only made her look grotesque?

Tears were beginning to threaten her vision when Clement said, "Do my eyes deceive me, or is this glamorous woman who just got into my car my erstwhile plain little cousin?"

A tremendous wave of relief flooded through her. But it was instantly followed by new doubts. Did he really mean what he'd said, or was he being sarcastic? With Clement Vaulkhurst, that was an ever-present possibility.

"What do you mean?" she asked, pretending innocence.

"You know very well what I mean! We leave you at this mall entrance a few hours ago, a plain young woman in sexless clothes, and I come back to find you transformed into a walking centerfold. Did some kind of good fairy wave her wand over you?"

He meant it! He was really impressed. He wasn't being sarcastic! Deborah felt an exultant flush of triumph surge through her from the tips of her toes to her face, turning her cheeks pink. Somehow she wasn't quite ready to analyze her feelings about it, but his response made the money she had spent worth every cent.

"No fairy godmother." She laughed, and the laughter bubbled up in her joyously, spontaneously. She didn't know when she had felt so happy in such a special way.

His eyes were twinkling. "You won't turn into a pumpkin at the stroke of midnight?"

She caught her breath and shook her head, smiling.

His gaze roved over her shamelessly, leaving little margin for modesty. She blushed again, and yet she felt pleased. His look was not merely an expression of lechery, though there was certainly an element of male sexual interest that quickened her pulse. But it was also a gaze of admiration, of approval, of surprise and wonder.

He slowly shook his head. "I really find this hard to believe. You know, you're full of surprises. That first night when I found you asleep on my doorstep, so to speak, you gave me the impression of a dowdy, inhibited little schoolgirl, totally shackled by convention. You first surprised me when you consented to become my unchaperoned houseguest. I didn't think you'd have the nerve to cast convention aside and accept my offer, but you did. And now, without warning, you suddenly emerge from your gray, sexless cocoon, a brilliant, gorgeous butterfly, What next, little cousin?"

Indeed—what next? The implications of that question made her heart flip over and stab her with sudden fright. She did not yet know the new, emerging Deborah Denhoff well enough to anticipate what other new experiences she might dare.

But, for now, she brought her thoughts back to the moment, savoring her triumph, basking in the glow of Clement's admiring gaze, feeling infinitely more feminine, from her smartly shod feet to the tips of her manicured nails, than she had ever felt before in her life.

"Well," said Clement, "I can only warn you that

now, more than ever, you remain in my household at your own risk. I'm sure you haven't transformed yourself into a sex goddess for your boyfriend, Bill Hughbank. He would be too myopic to appreciate the change!"

For a moment, her feeling of joy was shadowed by the old irritation at his colossal ego. "Certainly I did it for Bill. Any girl wants to look attractive for her boyfriend."

She challenged his amused, speculative gaze with a defiantly raised chin. But was she telling the truth? Uneasily, she did not want to answer that question, for in her heart she had to admit she had not given a moment's thought to Bill when she was picking out her new wardrobe, except for some qualms about his probably negative reaction.

Clement did not appear any more convinced by her words than she was herself. He merely chuckled.

Cars behind them were honking. Reluctantly, he withdrew his gaze from her and attended to his driving. "Serna is still at her hairdresser's. We'll pick her up now. It will be interesting to see what she thinks of your new appearance."

Interesting, indeed! Now that Clement's unqualified approval had bolstered her self-confidence, Deborah was looking forward to confronting the artist again. Now she felt they would meet on more equal terms, woman to woman.

And that was obviously Serna's reaction when they picked her up. She took a look at Deborah and paled noticeably; then her eyes flashed sparks. All the way during the two-hour drive back to Uromund she was in a black mood, making little effort to disguise the fact that she was boiling mad. Deborah had shot holes in her superior self-confidence by suddenly becoming equally attractive, something a woman could hardly forgive. When Serna spoke it was in terse monosyllables, and then she would lapse into brooding, sullen silence.

Deborah, on the other hand, felt high—deliciously intoxicated. All of her senses had become acute. The colors of the sky and pine trees were brilliant. The tires sang loudly on the pavement. Her nostrils quivered with the scent of her new perfume and the masculine smells of Clement's aftershave cologne and his pipe tobacco.

Deborah felt that she was in love with the world, in love with life, in love with herself. In love . . .

She glanced at Clement and a sudden sensation of fright shot through her again. All afternoon she had been trying to avoid facing her own heart. She kept coming back to it, like a moth to the flame; then, recognizing the danger, she fled from facing reality. The danger was real—as real as the flame that could burn her. But the truth had to be faced. She could hide from it just so long. Perhaps she had been hiding from it too long already. Had she been running away from her own heart since that first moment when she had gazed at the portrait of Clement Vaulkhurst and her emotions had become a raging storm?

Of course she hated him at times. Of course he infuriated her. Whatever emotions he stirred in her were violent. None of the passive, rational feelings she had for Bill Hughbank. Whenever there was a confrontation between her and Clement, her insides churned, her emotions convulsed, and she was left shaken and distraught. But she was also alive, feeling everything, whether it was desire or fury at him—alive down to her tingling nerve ends. Yes, Clement had the power to make her feel more alive in every way—for better or worse—than she had ever felt in the twenty-four years she had lived before she had met him. He had given her a taste of the shocking desire he could awaken in her.

And that was the major reason for the fright that possessed her now. Clement had said, "I can only warn you that now, more than ever, you remain in my household at your own risk." The warning echoed in her mind, sending an icy chill down her spine because it was absolutely true.

Yes, she was sure of it. She had to admit it. She had taken refuge in the old Deborah Denhoff. But the new person had been emerging within her, and she had been powerless as a crumbling dam to hold back all the new feelings, the new independence, the brand-new woman she was becoming.

And now the new woman, symbolized by the transformation she had made in her appearance this afternoon, had to face the truth about herself: She was in love with Clement!

Chapter Nine

Deborah spent a restless night, tossing and turning, dreaming fitfully, then enduring long hours of wakefulness, staring at the dark ceiling, trying to gain some rational control of her tumultuous emotions and a semblance of clear thought in her feverish mind.

She knew she must come to some conclusions about her future. How could she go on living in the Vaulkhurst mansion under these circumstances? It wasn't safe. She could no longer depend on her anger toward Clement to protect her from him—an anger that probably had been an unconscious defense she had used since the beginning. No, passion and desire had become too overpowering. Now that she faced the truth at last, that she was in love with Clement, she had no defenses left that she could rely upon.

And her feelings about Clement had not changed him. He was still Clement Vaulkhurst, as ruthless and dangerous as ever. Once he sensed surrender in her, he'd be quick to seize advantage of her new vulnerability. The warning Serna Czerny had given her now reechoed in her mind: "Clement is quite a villain where women are concerned, you know. He'll use you for his own selfish pleasure as long as he is amused and then toss you aside. . . ."

She had been angry with Serna at the time, but she knew there was truth in the warning—dangerous truth for her.

When dawn broke in a fiery ball through the pine trees, she had solved nothing. But she did know that she didn't wish to face Clement this morning. She didn't want to see Bill Hughbank or Serna Czerny or Clement's gardener, Andrew Smith, or the motel owner, Doug Carpenter. She did not want to have to deal with any of the people who had become a part of the drama in her life since she'd arrived in this town. She wanted to run and hide, for today at least.

Then she thought, What better place than to explore the Big Thicket? On her trip down here, she'd been excited about spending some time exploring this primitive area and adding to her bird-watching collection, but she'd become too embroiled with Clement and his book project. This morning would be a good time to steal for herself. Perhaps in the seclusion of the swampy forest, close to nature, she could confront the desires battling within herself and make some decisions.

She took a quick shower, ran a comb through her hair, donned blue jeans, boots, and a shirt, picked up her binoculars and camera bag, and slipped quietly downstairs.

The household was silent in this dawn hour. Last evening Clement had brought Deborah home, then he and Serna had driven off somewhere. She'd heard him return about midnight. Probably he'd be sleeping late this morning, which suited her plans very well. She let

herself quietly out of the mansion. She saw Andrew
Smith, who was apparently an early riser, clipping a
hedge along the rim of the garden. He straightened and
gave her a cheery wave, which she returned. Then she
backed her sports car out of the garage and minutes
later was driving down a dirt road, leaving a cloud of
dust behind.

It was a spectacular morning. The sun, wild and fiery
red, was just clearing the rim of the forest. To the north
and east, thunderheads were piled like white pillows
against a black sky. There were distant flashes of
lightning and a faint muttering of thunder. But the
storm clouds were far enough away that she doubted
they would threaten her morning adventure.

She had traveled this road once before on a round-
about drive from town and had noticed an old deserted
road left behind by a lumbering company jutting off
into the swamp. A sign, *Nature Trail,* had been placed
beside the lumber-camp road.

She soon arrived at the spot and turned into the lane.
Suddenly, she found herself in a world as remote from
civilization as a tangled jungle in the Amazon. The only
clue that a human being had been here before herself
was the rutted lane she was driving on, and it grew
fainter as she followed it deeper into the marshy
thicket. Apparently, the road had not been used in a
long time, for weeds had grown up, obscuring the ruts.
Now she was skirting great swampy areas where broken
and dead tree stumps rose from the gray water like the
bones of prehistoric monsters. An early-morning mist
shrouded the marshy ground, giving a ghostly, eerie
appearance to her surroundings. Her car rattled over a
small, rickety bridge. The sound startled what looked
like a brown log in the mud beside a swamp. The log

turned out to be an alligator that went slithering into
the stagnant water with a soft splash.

Deborah shuddered and put a few more hundred
yards between herself and that spot. Then she stopped
beside a huge cypress tree. When she switched off the
engine, silence fell upon her like a blanket. Then,
gradually, she became aware of the sounds of the
forest, the call of a distant bird, the rustle of an unseen
animal in the underbrush, the ripple of something—a
snake or alligator—moving through the swamp. The air
was musky with the heavy odor of rotting wood,
stagnant water, and lush undergrowth. But there was
also mingled with it the fragrance of native flowers
growing in wild profusion.

Excited at the prospect of seeing exotic bird specimens to add to her collection, Deborah gathered up her
binoculars and camera and slid out of her car. She
found a footpath leading from the lane between pools
of swampy water. She followed the path, wondering
what kind of animals had made it. A shiver ran through
her when she realized that a panther or a wild bear
might have trod this same path only last night. She
made a mental note not to wander too far from her car.

She had spent some summers with her father exploring South American jungles in search of archaeological
ruins, so she did not consider herself a total novice in
this primitive setting. It did not hold the terror for her it
would have had for a total amateur who had never been
out of an urban environment.

As she began scanning the trees with her binoculars,
she realized she had instinctively made the right choice
in coming here. The quiet peacefulness of nature was
seeping into her being like a tranquilizer, soothing her
nerves and settling her frayed emotions. It was the

perfect antidote for the storm that had been raging
inside her. For the first time since yesterday's unsettling
discoveries about herself and her true feeling about
Clement, she felt a measure of calmness.

Since time's beginning, the human heart has found
peace in the rhythm of the oceans, the solitude of the
mountains, and the quietness of the forests. She
remembered the words of the psalm, "I will lift up mine
eyes unto the hills from whence cometh my help." She
had not gone to the hills, but she had gone in search of
solitude in this remote setting and had found renewed
spiritual strength here.

With the growing peace in her heart came rational
thought. She had not quite made her decision about her
future, but she felt a growing resolve that she was not
going to throw her life away by plunging recklessly into
an emotional whirlpool with Clement. She did love
him. Nothing would change that. But she knew she
must face the fact that loving Clement Vaulkhurst was a
trap, a dead-end street leading nowhere but to a blank
wall of disaster, and she must act accordingly. She
would not be the first woman who kept a hopeless love
a secret forever locked in her heart.

She was so engrossed in her thoughts and her bird
watching that she was not aware of the increasing
rumble of thunder. She had fitted a zoom lens on her
single-lens reflex camera that ranged from 90 mm. to
250 mm. and was snapping some exciting color shots of
birds. She became aware of the growing darkness when
her between-the-lens light meter indicated a need for
wider and wider apertures. She glanced upward and
realized that the sun was being hidden by dark clouds.
The forest was becoming shrouded in midday twilight
and had grown hushed. Birds had stopped singing, and

the jungle around her appeared to be holding its breath in anticipation of an approaching storm.

Then there was a crash of thunder so close it startled her. She accepted that as a signal that her bird-watching expedition was over for the day. And she suddenly realized that she had skipped breakfast and was becoming ravenous. She put her binoculars in their case and snapped it shut and tucked her camera equipment in her shoulder bag, then started back to her car. She had gone only halfway when raindrops began splattering on leaves around her. The drops had turned into a downpour by the time she reached her car. Shivering and wet, she put the top up. Then she piled in and started the engine.

The thunderstorm struck with torrential ferocity. Great sheets of water were dumped splashing through the trees. It was like driving through a continuous waterfall. She could not see past the front of her little car which slithered bravely down a lane that was rapidly turning into a river of mud.

Then her heart sank as she heard a high-pitched whine of the back tires spinning helplessly. She was stuck.

She tried rocking the car back and forth, but only succeeded in sinking more deeply into the mud until it was up to her hubcaps. Then she switched off the engine and looked around, assaying her situation with a sense of frustration and despair. But she told herself there was no reason to panic. She was in no immediate danger. True, she was stuck here, but she wasn't going to drown. And she was hungry, but she wouldn't starve. A person, she knew, could survive for days without food. The worst that could happen was that she'd be uncomfortable for a while.

She decided to wait until the rain eased up, then begin walking. That took more time than she anticipated. The storm had settled into a steady downpour that showed little signs of abating. By midafternoon, her stomach was cramping with hunger, and she was beside herself with boredom and frustration. She realized that the rain could easily continue for several days. She had no desire to spend the night here with water rising around her and snakes slithering through the swamp, perhaps crawling into her car.

She wished now she had paid more attention to the threatening weather, but she realized that chiding herself wasn't going to solve her dilemma. She gathered her courage, took a deep breath, and stepped out into the rain. Resolutely, she began walking. The mud sucked at her boots. She slipped and staggered through the swampy mire. Before she'd gone ten feet, she was soaked to the skin. She shivered and wept as the rain plastered her hair, ruining the expensive new styling.

She couldn't remember ever having been so cold, wet, hungry, and miserable. But she thought she must plow doggedly on if she was going to reach the main road before dark.

Suddenly there was a brilliant flash of lightning, a clap of thunder that deafened her, the smell of sulfur, and an ear-splitting crash. She screamed, seeing a giant tree only a few hundred yards ahead of her split apart by a bolt of lightning. The charred, blackened limbs hissed and spluttered in the rain.

Almost instantly, there was another thunderous crash nearby. The earth shook. Deborah fell to her knees in the mud, covering her ears, sobbing hysterically. She felt like a soldier caught helplessly in an artillery barrage. She was in the center of an electric storm!

Lightning was felling trees all around her. The electric charge in the air was so intense that the hair on the back of her neck stood up.

Never had she been so terrified. She thought that she was surely going to die here in this desolate swamp all alone. Her body might not be found for weeks, and by then wild animals would have torn it apart. She sobbed and prayed with a sense of utter aloneness in a terrifying, primitive universe.

Suddenly, something was coming toward her. A gray, bumping monster with eyes glowing like fire. She screamed again.

And then the monster slowed to a stop in front of her. The glowing eyes became headlights. The gleaming skin became the steel fenders of a four-wheel-drive vehicle. A door slammed, and a figure dressed in a rain slicker and rubber boots ran to her and gathered her up in powerful arms.

Through the tears and rain that half blinded her, she made out dark, familiar features. Clement roared over the thunder of the storm, "You little idiot! Are you trying to drown yourself?"

They drove back to where she'd abandoned her car and hooked a tow chain to it. Andrew Smith, who was with Clement in the Jeep, steered Deborah's car as they pulled it out of the mud. Then Andrew drove her car home. Clement followed, driving the Jeep, with Deborah a huddled, soggy mass beside him.

Clement fussed at her all the way back to the mansion. "Don't you know people go into that swamp and are never heard of again?"

"H-how did you ever find me?" she asked through chattering teeth.

"Andrew saw you leave this morning with your binoculars and camera. When the storm hit, we called around town and the motel, but nobody had seen you today. We deduced that you'd ventured into the Thicket. Lucky for you, Andrew and I know this swamp as well as any two people in the county. There aren't many roads around here that an amateur bird watcher could take to go venturing into that area. We tried them all—and luckily found you."

He glared at her. "I'd turn you over my knee and give you a spanking you'd never forget for going into that area without a guide and without telling anyone where you were headed . . . except, from the looks of you, I'd say you've been punished enough! You look like a half-drowned kitten." He roared with laughter.

She thought that if she weren't so grateful for being rescued, she'd wish one of those lightning bolts would strike him!

When they arrived at Clement's mansion, Deborah went to her room. Chilled to the bone, she shed her soggy clothes and soaked in a hot tub until she was finally warm again. She dried briskly with a rough towel, did what she could to repair her hair style, and then wrapped up in a soft bathrobe.

There was a knock at her bedroom door. She opened it, and Clement, standing in the hallway, said, "I thought your little adventure might have given you an appetite, so Andrew and I have been busy in the kitchen."

Delicious aromas wafted from the silver tray Clement was holding. He brought it into her room and arranged it on a table. When he uncovered the dishes, she saw a golden omelette, crisp bacon, piles of toast, jelly, a bowl of fresh fruit, and a pot of rich, steaming coffee.

"The coffee is my idea," Clement said, "Andrew is a hot-tea nut, but I insisted you needed a more restorative brew."

Deborah took a sip of the coffee, coughed, and blinked.

"Oh, I put some brandy in it," Clement explained.

More like you put some coffee in the brandy, she thought.

Then he sprawled comfortably in a chair and lit his pipe while Deborah eagerly attacked the meal. Between mouthfuls, she glanced at him. He was puffing contentedly on his pipe, watching her with an amused expression. "Don't eat the dishes."

"This is delicious," she said. She piled mounds of butter and marmalade on her toast. "I'm just starved."

"So I notice."

"I left without eating breakfast this morning."

"Another idiotic thing to do. You need a keeper."

She was too busy enjoying the meal to let his remark irritate her.

At last, having cleaned up every morsel from the plates and licked the jam from her fingers, she sighed and settled back in her chair. "Oh, I feel ever so much better. I didn't think I'd ever be dry and comfortable again."

Clement tapped the tobacco from his pipe into an ashtray. He cleared his throat. "I was worried about you," he muttered.

She looked at him with surprise. "Somehow I can't imagine you being worried about anyone."

"Yes, well, you don't know me very well." He rose

and moved restlessly about the room. "You don't know me at all, as a matter of fact."

"I'll have to agree with that," she admitted. "Who does? You are a complex and enigmatic man. But I do know you are self-centered and ego-oriented, as are most highly creative people. It's just surprising that you'd spend any of your valuable time worrying about someone else."

"Now you're being sarcastic."

"I didn't mean it that way—"

"I'm as human as you are!" he exploded. "Of course I think about other people, worry about them, grieve over them. I'm quite capable of weeping for the entire pitiful, tragic human race, and often do, as a matter of fact—"

He broke off and stood scowling out the window at the gray, dripping sky.

"I—I wish you wouldn't say things like that . . ." She faltered.

"Why?"

"Because," she whispered, "it makes you terribly attractive. I—I don't think you often let people see the human side of you this way. . . ."

He turned and looked at her in a peculiar, searching manner. She flushed and dropped her gaze. The room fell silent. She could hear the patter of raindrops against the window and the pounding of her own heart.

He moved across the room and gently held her in his arms. She felt a tremor run through her body, but it was not from being cold. She felt warm all over; her face was flushed.

"Deborah, I *was* worried about you . . . almost

beside myself, to be completely truthful. I think this is the time to tell you that you have become very important to me. More than I had realized. I think I was jolted into the truth about my feelings for you that night in the garden when I saw Bill Hughbank kissing you. I felt he was violating something precious that belonged to me. I had the impulse to smash him for touching you . . ."

"Please—" she stammered, her emotions raging again.

"No, I have to tell you this. You are no longer a naïve schoolgirl who amuses me. I've seen you turn into a woman before my eyes—a very desirable woman. I want you desperately, Deborah. And I know you feel the same about me. Don't deny it. I've felt the response in you when I've kissed you. I've felt you tremble with desire."

He kissed her now, more gently than the times before, but igniting the same responding fire in her body.

She closed her eyes, letting his kiss overwhelm her for a delicious moment, but then she drew back from his arms. She breathed deeply, grasping desperately for sanity. "So now you want me—"

"Yes," he said roughly. "I want you to move out of this ridiculous guest room and into my room. We'll make a wonderful pair, Deborah. When we finish my novel, we'll take a year off to see the world. We'll hold hands in a London fog, sip champagne in a sidewalk café in Paris, watch the sun set over the Nile. . . ."

"'A wonderful pair . . .'" she repeated. "You mean a *ménage à trois,* don't you?"

"What are you talking about?"

"You seem to have conveniently forgotten Serna. Or has she just been fired as your mistress?"

He frowned at her. "What makes you think she *is* my mistress?"

Deborah gasped. "Are you going to deny it?"

"Yes," he said flatly.

"I thought this was a moment of truth between us."

"It is. Serna is a dear old friend, nothing more."

Deborah said, her eyes blazing, "I suppose you are going to tell me you are not sleeping with your 'dear old friend!'"

"Yes, that's exactly what I'm telling you."

"How about that day I was in the study typing? You brought Serna here in the afternoon, and then you and she went up to your room. Later, you came down to the pool where I was swimming. Are you going to tell me you hadn't been making love to Serna?" she challenged.

"Well, that's exactly what I'm going to tell you. We were not in my room at all. I have another workroom upstairs. Serna is doing the artwork for the jacket on my new novel. We were up there discussing some sketches she's working on. I heard you splashing about downstairs in the pool and went down to join you."

Deborah stared at him openmouthed. Could she believe him? But his lifelong friend, Andrew Smith, who knew him as well as anyone, had told her what an accomplished liar Clement could be.

"Serna seems to have a different view of your relationship with her. She warned me to stay away from you . . . that you belonged to her."

"Oh, yes. Serna can be quite possessive. It's true that we had a bit of a romantic fling a long time ago, when she first came to the United States. It was brief and, as far as I'm concerned, has been over for a long, long time. But Serna can't quite accept that. She'd still like the world to believe that she is the mistress of Clement Vaulkhurst. I think it's more a matter of her ego than any real feeling she has for me. Gives her a touch of international fame, which she craves."

"But—but I saw you kiss her in the garden that night after the dinner—"

He chuckled. "And you were jealous. So that explains why you got yourself all wrapped up in Bill Hughbank's embrace . . . for my benefit!"

Her face reddened. "Don't change the subject. You *were* kissing Serna."

"Yes, indeed," he admitted, "but it meant nothing. I was thanking Serna for helping arrange the dinner. Actually, it was Serna doing most of the kissing. As I said, we're old friends, and old friends sometimes kiss. It meant no more than a handshake."

He was getting her confused. She turned away, frowning. "You never said before that you were just friends. You seemed to enjoy flaunting her at me—"

"Only because I could see it made you jealous." He chuckled. "And that amused me. But I'm not in the mood for any more childish games."

Suddenly, he was holding her, his fierce, black-eyed gaze reaching into the depths of her being like a scorching flame. "You want me, too, little Deborah. I know it. Why go on denying the hunger we feel for each other?"

With an effort, she drew her eyes from his hypnotic gaze. She pressed her palms against her throbbing temples. "Clement, please. Don't rush me at a time like this. I've been through a nerve-racking, harrowing experience. I'm exhausted and my nerves are shot. I'm in no condition to cope with a situation like this that is going to change my entire life. I need to rest . . . to get myself back together—"

He nodded, his face sober. "You're right, of course. I could have picked a better time. But I was desperately worried when the storm struck and we knew you were out in that treacherous swamp all alone. I couldn't stop from telling you how I feel about you and how much I want you."

He bent and kissed her tenderly. "You have a rest now. Have a good night's sleep. We'll have a lot of tomorrows to share together."

How self-confident he was! He knew full well her weakness for him, that his touch could dissolve her resistance as if it were a wisp of smoke. He took it for granted she'd accept his proposition.

She needed to get him out of her bedroom before she lost what little reason she had left now. And, fortunately, he did leave.

When he was gone, she paced the room for a while, then lay across the bed, staring at the ceiling. Tears were trickling from her eyes. She whispered aloud the things she'd been too weak to say to his face. "What you say is true, Clement. I won't deny I don't have the same feeling for you. Yes, I am in love with you, and I want you. I've already admitted that to myself. But it isn't enough. I'm sorry, Clement, but I also know this is just going to lead to heartbreak for me. I'll always be grateful that you've helped bring me out of my shell. You've gotten me over a lot of the rigid conventions that kept me so inhibited and unfulfilled as a person.

But there is one thing I can never change. Love for me has to mean total commitment to a man for a lifetime, and that includes exchanging marriage vows."

She smiled tearfully. "I'm afraid, in that area, I'm still as conventional as ever," she whispered, continuing her tearful monologue. "I happen to believe in institutions like marriage and family. I'm sorry if that makes me sound old-fashioned, but I think our civilization depends on those values. At least I know my self-respect and happiness and security depend on them. . . ."

Clement had said that he was attracted to her, that he wanted her. Not once had he used the word love. Not once had he mentioned a wedding ceremony. "Move into my room." That had been his proposition. Clearly a proposition, not a proposal—an invitation to sleep with him, a temporary affair, not a lifetime commitment.

Perhaps he did care for her right now. Spending a year with him traveling around the world would be a romantic dream. But what would become of her when the dream ended . . . when he grew tired of her? This was only a temporary conquest for him; otherwise he would have asked her to marry him.

She thought about the spiritual peace she had found in the solitude of the forest. Now she recaptured that mood until she felt calm and strong inside.

She spent the next hour composing a letter for Clement. She lacked the courage to give him her answer to his face. She was afraid that at a look from him, a touch of his hand, she would weaken.

In her letter she tried to write down the words she had been saying aloud. She could not deny that a year with him would contain more excitement, more passion, more fulfillment than many women know in a lifetime. Yet, she could not settle for a temporary love affair, no matter how alluring. She was the marrying kind, a one-man woman who needed from her man the moral and spiritual foundation of marriage and family. She wanted children. In that respect, she and Clement were still worlds apart.

Sadly, she dressed and packed her bags, knowing that she was leaving behind all her aspirations of literary achievement, along with the man she loved. The summer was going to have a sad ending for her, yet it would be an ending she could live with. She could never live with herself as Clement's newest romantic fling. She would destroy herself and in the end destroy the passion that had brought them together, or Clement would tire of her when a new attraction came along. In either case, their relationship would be doomed from the beginning.

Other women have recovered from impossible loves and broken hearts. She must do the same.

She left the letter where he would find it and, for the second time that day, stole out of the house. Darkness had fallen. Too exhausted by the day's events to drive farther than town, she took a cabin at Doug Carpenter's motel for the night. Like a bloodhound on the scent of fresh gossip, the motel owner eagerly plied her with questions. But she cut him short and went to her room. There, she fell into bed and was asleep in minutes.

Early the next morning, there came an urgent knock at her cabin door. She came awake all at once, flinging the bedclothes back. The first thought that raced through her mind was that it was Clement. He'd read her letter this morning and had rushed here to tell her that he couldn't bear to lose her and would gladly marry her. But a second, more logical thought quickly pushed that fantasy aside. More likely it was Bill Hughbank, who had heard from the motel owner that she had checked in here last night. No doubt Doug Carpenter had served him that bit of information with his early-morning free coffee.

"Just a minute," she called out. She slipped into a robe and went to the door.

Yes, it was Bill.

When she opened the door, he rushed in looking agitated and concerned. "Are you all right, Deborah?" he demanded. "I just found out you checked in here last night. Did Vaulkhurst try to attack you or something? I wouldn't put anything past that man. You never should have moved into his home without someone to protect you—"

She couldn't help smiling at Bill's agitation. "Calm down, Bill, for heaven's sake. No, Clement didn't do anything to me. I'm perfectly all right."

"Well, thank goodness for that," he said with genuine relief. He drew her into his arms and held her in a warm, secure embrace.

Suddenly she felt weary of battling with Clement, with Serna, with Bill, with her parents, and mostly with her own emotions. It was good to feel the security of a man's protective arms around her . . . a man who could make life quite simple for her. With Bill she didn't have to agonize over moral decisions, fight primitive emotions, be shocked at her own traitorous desires. Bill represented a sane, secure, predictable life. He didn't ask her to move into his bedroom, to simply cast aside all the moral restraints of a lifetime and go dashing off around the world on a yearlong love affair. He wanted to marry her, to help him establish a home, and to have children. "'Till death us do part . . .'": the words of the wedding ceremony she had dreamed of all her life as most girls do.

Was that the reason she had stopped here at the motel last night instead of driving farther on? She had told herself it was because she was too tired to drive farther, and that was partly true; but, unconsciously, she had probably gone to the place where Bill was staying because she knew he would offer her refuge. Going back to Bill was like returning to her family and her safe home, and after what she had been through yesterday, that didn't seem so bad.

Now she was going to have to swallow her stubborn pride. "You're right, Bill," she sighed. "I guess you've been right all along. This trip to Uromund has been a wild-goose chase. My parents tried to talk me out of it and so did you, but I wouldn't listen—"

She suddenly felt dangerously close to tears. She moved away from his arms and got hold of herself with an effort. How humiliating it was going to be to return home, to admit to her parents, to her brilliant brother and sister, to her English professor, that she had failed to write the biographical thesis on Clement Vaulkhurst. Of course, she couldn't tell them the real reason she had abandoned the project.

True, she still had the early writings and memorabilia of Clement's that she had obtained from Aunt Christina. It would be possible for her to use that plus what she had learned from being so close to him these past weeks to put together some kind of thesis about him on her own. But it would be too painful. Right now she couldn't think about him without tears scorching her eyes, much less write about him. No, she would return the material to Aunt Christina and then begin the painful healing process of forgetting Clement Vaulkhurst.

"What happened?" Bill demanded, breaking into her thoughts.

She tried to organize her mind. Bill deserved an explanation. She could tell him no less than the truth.

She sank on the edge of the bed, fumbling with the cord of her robe as she sought the right words. "Well . . . it started yesterday morning. Like an idiot, I went bird watching as the storm was coming up and got stuck in the swamp. Clement and his gardener, Andrew Smith, went searching for me in a Jeep and fortunately they found me. They took me back to Clement's house. Then—" She felt her cheeks grow warm. "Well, this part isn't easy, but you are entitled to know the truth, Bill. Clement has become infatuated with me. I—I guess that's the word to use. He told me he wants me to—to leave on a world tour with him after he finishes his novel—"

Bill blinked at her. "He wants you to marry him?"

"I didn't seem to hear any mention of marriage in the proposal," she said grimly. "In fact, I don't think 'proposal' is exactly the proper term to use."

Hughbank flushed angrily. "I knew it! I knew all along what kind of rat that man is. I ought to go out and smash him on the jaw."

"Oh, Bill, don't go sounding like a hero in a Gay

Nineties melodrama, wanting to thrash the villain for besmirching the pure heroine's honor! This is the twentieth century. We both know a lot of couples live together these days without going through the formality of a wedding ceremony. I just don't happen to be quite that unconventional. I've shed a lot of my old inhibitions these past weeks, but I still do believe in marriage, at least for me. I want children. I can understand the kind of man Clement is—unshackled, independent, living by his own rules. . . ."

"Well, I'll agree with what you said about how you've changed," Bill admitted. "Sometimes I hardly know you anymore. But I'm glad to hear you still have some old-fashioned virtues left."

Bill was pacing around the room, obviously struggling with his own inner conflict. Finally he said, "There is one thing you haven't told me, Deborah. I think you should be honest with me about this, too—how do you feel about Clement Vaulkhurst? Obviously you turned down his proposition, since you left his household. But what if he'd asked you to marry him?" He was standing over her now, his gaze searching and demanding.

She had been dreading this question. Should she be totally honest with Bill? Would anything be gained by hurting him needlessly? She'd already put him through enough turmoil to make her feel terribly guilty—although, being honest with herself, she knew she hadn't asked him to come down here; he'd made that move on his own. As for her feelings about Clement, they were a private matter, and she was still in such a turmoil about them that she couldn't clearly put them into words without a great deal of pain—and didn't want to try. "Bill, I can assure you nothing serious happened between Clement and me while I was his houseguest. Now I'm relieved to be away from him, and I just want to go home. . . ."

If that was being evasive, it was the best she could do in her present state of mind. Fortunately, it appeared to satisfy Bill. Perhaps, she thought, he really didn't want to probe too deeply into her feelings about Clement for fear of what might be uncovered. She was out of Clement's household, and that gave him the upper hand.

Perhaps he thought that once he got her away from the influence of Clement Vaulkhurst and back home, whatever feelings she'd had for the novelist would fade away. And right now, she hoped the same thing.

Bill spent the rest of the morning getting her car ready for the trip back home. He took it to a service station to have the swamp mud washed off and have the automobile greased and tuned up.

Deborah dressed for the trip home. All morning she wondered if Clement was going to let her leave without saying a word. In the letter she'd told him she was going to the motel for the night and would leave for home the next day. She thought any minute the phone would ring or he would knock on her door. Her traitorous heart clung to the faint hope that he would come here at the last minute, sweep her into his arms, declare his love for her and his willingness to make her his bride.

But that moment never came. And when Bill brought the car back at noon and said they were ready to leave, the last hope died quietly in her breast. By his silence, Clement had made it crystal clear that he had no intention of marrying her, that, just as she'd supposed, he wanted her only to satisfy his lust for her . . . a temporary arrangement that would end when he tired of her. . . .

As they drove away from Uromund, Deborah looked back once through her tears and in her heart whispered, *Goodbye, my love. . . .*

Chapter Ten

The remainder of the summer was soon gone. The trees on the university campus were changing color in an early autumn as the fall term began.

Bill Hughbank arrived one evening to take Deborah out for a dinner date. "Mario's okay?" he asked, opening his car door for her.

"Sure," she replied with an inward smile at Bill's predictability. He invariably suggested the Italian restaurant when he had some important news to tell her. She could even guess with a fair degree of certainty what the news was this time.

Bill hummed softly as he drove. He looked extremely pleased with himself.

Deborah mused, Should I wait until we get to the restaurant, or get him to tell me now? It was obvious that Bill was hardly able to contain himself. All it would take would be a word from her. . . .

She nibbled at her lip for a moment, then said in a casual manner, "Weren't you due to take your bar exam this past week?"

A grin broke out. He said, "Yes, and I passed it with flying colors. I was going to wait and tell you over a bottle of wine at Mario's, but you might as well hear the news now. I've been accepted into my father's law firm as a junior partner!"

"Bill, that's marvelous! Congratulations! You worked so hard, and you deserve it."

She felt a genuine warmth and happiness for his success, but at the same time a part of her wondered if the rest of her life with Bill was going to be this predictable. There were no surprises where Bill was concerned. She almost knew what his next sentence was going to be when they talked. Perhaps that was as it should be. A safe, rational companionship. No thrilling, unexpected surprises—but no crushing disappointments, either. Just nice, smooth sailing down a carefully plotted course.

Bill had been driving up from New York to see her at least once a week since they had returned from Uromund. By mutual, unspoken agreement, they never talked about what had happened there. But it remained between them, a silent mocking shadow staining their relationship.

Those weeks at Uromund had left an indelible mark on Deborah. She had come back changed, unwilling to surrender the measure of self-confidence she had gained along with the sense of having become an adult.

She knew the change in her was making Bill confused and unhappy, and she was sorry about that. She was trying to adjust. She knew that he, too, was making a valiant attempt to cope with their changed relationship.

The fact that they were going through a difficult period of adjustment had kept their engagement plans nebulous. They had talked about making a formal announcement early in the fall, but Deborah shied away from thinking about a specific date.

They both realized their relationship had changed. Had they simply become resigned to going ahead with their engagement plans?

Mario's was the kind of restaurant that strived a bit too self-consciously to create an Italian atmosphere. Candles dripped wax down old Chianti bottles as they cast flickering, shadowy light. The tablecloths were checkered, of course, and vines entwined their way up latticework. But Deborah suspected that the cook was Brooklyn-born of Latin-American extraction and presided over the kitchen with an Italian cookbook in one hand.

"Veal scallopini," Bill told the aproned waiter after they were seated. "Antipasto. And red wine."

After the waiter had brought the wine, Bill touched his glass against Deborah's. "To us." He smiled.

"Yes," she said. "To us."

She sipped the heavy wine, glancing across the table at Bill. He looked flushed, bright-eyed, and handsome. She searched her heart for her true feelings about him. Was she fond of him? Yes, of course. In love? She didn't want to answer that question now. But did she want to be his wife? Yes, she thought; they could have a good marriage. Bill was as eager as she to have children. That was important.

Bill had fallen silent. He looked pensive. Was he also questioning his feelings about her? she wondered. This strained, uneasy feeling came between them often, lately. Perhaps, she thought, it was part of the adjustment they were experiencing. They were both doing some deep soul-searching, floundering for some kind of solid ground they could stand on together.

"How are you getting along with your parents these days?" Bill asked suddenly. "I suppose your mother can't quite get used to the way you want to take over and handle things yourself now."

Deborah nodded soberly. "Yes. I'm afraid she's both disconcerted and baffled by her youngest daughter who suddenly isn't a child anymore."

A shadow crossed Bill's face. "You *have* changed, Deborah. I—I was worried for a while—"

She gave him a searching look, hoping they could bring their feelings into the open and somehow resolve their problems together. "What do you mean?"

"Well, at first after we came back from Uromund, you were so strong-willed. Remember the spats we had over little things? I was beginning to worry about whether we were doing the right thing about plans for our future together. But lately you do seem a bit more like your old self. I'm sure after we're married and settle down, you'll be the old Deborah I've always known."

Deborah felt a chill. Somehow that wasn't what she'd hoped he would say. The old Deborah . . .? The stifled, conventional, inhibited, fearful Deborah? Was that what Bill really wanted? Even worse, was that what she was becoming again?

A shudder ran through her. "Heaven forbid, Bill. You don't really want me like that." But her voice lacked conviction and faltered when she saw the pensive, questioning expression on his face again.

The conversation was making her uneasy, so she changed the subject, talking about Bill's new position with his father's law firm.

Once, during the meal, she glanced up from her plate

as a couple across the room left their table. The man was tall and powerfully built. He had a shock of dark, unruly hair. For a second Deborah's heart changed tempo, her breath caught in her throat.

How long was it going to be like this? she wondered. How many times in the coming years was she going to see a man who resembled Clement and feel her mind go blank and the pain in the secret corner of her heart throb? How many times would she remember—and the remembering bring an aching void? How many women were there, she wondered, who had considerate husbands, loving children, safe, happy homes, and yet carried their silent memory of a passionate, lost love, and at times thought sadly of what might have been?

She remembered a verse she'd heard as a child and tried to recall how it went, "Of all sad words of tongue or pen, the saddest are these: 'It might have been. . . .'"

Her mind turned back to the events of this past summer after she and Bill left Uromund. They had driven back to Connecticut in an uneventful trip. She had felt like a sleepwalker returning to reality after a lengthy, disturbing dream. But, while dreaming, she had somehow changed and was like a stranger returning to the familiar university campus.

Once Bill had brought her safely home, he had gone on to New York to visit his family and make preparations to take his bar examination. He had left Deborah to make her own painful readjustment to reality. There had not been a moment on the long drive home that she had not thought about Clement and wondered how she could live from day to day without the excitement that being near him had made flow through her veins. The hurting inside her was deeper than she had thought it would be. She wondered how long it would be before the bright edge of pain and loss would begin to fade.

Somehow, she had concealed her feelings from Bill, holding them privately in her heart, while she maintained a casual exterior. She was grateful for Bill at a time like this. He bolstered her courage, and his talk about their wedding plans and the home they were going to buy gave her something to think about and to distract her. But they were not entirely comfortable with each other. Deborah's mind kept wandering, and Bill seemed disconcerted by the changes this summer had made in her personality. Would they be permanent changes? she wondered. The more she was with Bill and the closer she came to home, the more she felt the new and old Deborahs battling inside her.

Once home, her first task had been to contact her mother and her father. She was panic-stricken at the thought of explaining, when they returned to the campus at the end of summer, why she had dropped the Clement Vaulkhurst biographical thesis project. She was too humiliated to tell them the real reason. No, she decided, she would write to them and merely say that they had been right, that Clement was an impossible person to deal with, and the whole project had become so unpleasant that she had decided to abandon it.

She was pleased with herself when she reread the letters. She hadn't actually lied. Clement, in a sense, had been an impossible person to deal with. He had wanted her for a temporary bed partner; she had wanted marriage and children, and so they couldn't agree. Of course, she didn't put that part in the letters, and her parents would put a different interpretation on her words. That would be fine. The letters would get her off the hook. And her mother and father were too civilized to remind her that they had told her so. Knowing them as she did, she felt sure the matter would be dropped, and they'd say nothing at all about it when they returned.

The head of her English department was understanding about her decision to drop the Vaulkhurst project. "I have to tell you I'm disappointed somewhat, Deborah. You were so enthusiastic about it, and I really thought you might pull it off since you are related to Clement Vaulkhurst. But never mind. We can agree on another topic for your thesis, I'm sure."

For the time being, Deborah had not the stomach to do any more work on her master's degree. Perhaps later she might feel in the mood to take it up again. But now, it only reminded her of how bright and shining her summer had started out, and how all her dreams had turned to dust.

When Deborah's parents returned from their respective summer assignments, Deborah felt the old fences closing in around her again. It was with a wave of anxiety that she realized her new independence wasn't going to be easy to hold on to. Here in the university life, in the home of her parents, she found it hard to remember how she had become her own person those exciting weeks in Uromund.

Deborah thought it had been a strange paradox that when she'd had Clement for a catalyst, it had been easier for her to make up her own mind and live her own life. As overpowering as he was, he had somehow aroused the courage in her to stand up to him. Perhaps a little of the way he had not given a damn what the world thought of him had rubbed off on her.

Her parents and friends on the campus had certainly

been aware of the change in her when she returned from Uromund. Most apparent, of course, had been the change in her appearance. Her glamorous new hair style and wardrobe had surprised everyone. Her mother had looked at her a little like a mother hen who sat on her egg and was startled to see a peacock hatch out.

The metamorphosis had begun before summer vacation, when she'd announced her plans to go to Uromund. But there were other, deeper changes now.

"You've become quite—grown up. Quite mature, Deborah," her mother had remarked. "You're a woman . . . no longer my little girl. I must confess I don't feel I know you as well as I used to."

And yet Deborah felt her new maturity being endangered by the old inhibitions and restraints that threatened to overtake her again. It was as if a cloud were following her and getting ready to settle over her life forever. With the cloud came feelings of confusion, doubt, and anxiety. She had not felt that cloud in Uromund. There she had felt free to be herself, to make her own decisions and suffer the consequences of her own behavior. She had been strictly on her own, and while the feeling had been scary in some ways, she had felt totally alive and had relished the feeling.

But now she had Bill to think about. She knew she wasn't passionately in love with him as she had been with Clement. But he would be a good husband, and she would make him a good wife. They would have children. In time, she would learn to love Bill. Probably it would never be the burning, chaotic, blind passion she felt for Clement. But it would be a steady, faithful, companionable affection. The part of her that would always belong to Clement would forever be a secret locked in her heart, a memory that would be with her the rest of her life.

But being Bill's wife meant change. It meant submerging her life into his. That brought new conflicts. If she rebelled against convention too much, or displayed independence beyond a certain measure, it displeased and upset him. She wasn't entirely sure how she was going to handle that.

The remainder of their dinner at Mario's passed in a mood of pleasant companionship with Bill. They kept their conversation light and impersonal, which seemed the safest ground for the time being.

"Don't forget," she reminded him when he kissed her good night, "we're having the faculty reception next weekend. You promised you'd be here."

"Yes, I can make it," he assured her.

On Tuesday night, Deborah's mother and father went to a university faculty business meeting, leaving Deborah home alone. She had settled down with a book for company when, shortly before nine o'clock, the phone rang.

She answered and a familiar, deep voice demanded, "Deborah? Is that you?"

Her hand was suddenly a frozen clamp, holding the telephone. Her breath caught in her throat. In that first moment of stunned surprise, her mind was a wasteland. Shattered fragments of questions were scattered in the wind. Clement, calling her after all these weeks? Why—*why?* A hope that had been laid to rest in a secret corner of her heart stirred to life. Her own treacherous heart had not changed. The sound of his voice had her pulse racing.

His voice rattled the telephone receiver. "Well, speak up, little cousin. Have you fainted?"

She moistened her lips, swallowed hard. "Very nearly," she said weakly. "I—I certainly didn't expect to hear from you again."

"I daresay. Well, what are you doing now?"

"What—what do you mean?"

"Well, are you going back to school or trying to write a thesis or whatever it is?" Then he said ominously, "You didn't write my biography without my permission, did you?"

"Certainly not!" she retorted with an unexpected flash of anger, reminded again how infuriating he could be. "I have no intention of writing about you. Why did you call, anyway?"

He chuckled. "From the sound of your voice, you still have strong feelings for me. Good. Now, tell me, why did you run off like a coward? I gave you credit for more character than that."

"Character!" She gasped. "You're a fine one to talk about 'character'! You know good and well why I left. I explained it in very clear and simple language in the note I left. You do, occasionally, read something besides your own manuscripts, I assume?"

"Not usually. I find most other reading material, except for some works by the masters, quite boring. Your note was extremely boring. Very poorly composed. Melodramatic and emotional. Extremely illogical, to boot."

She blinked back hurting tears. "I'd almost forgotten how despicable and heartless you can be if you choose! I laid my heart bare in that note."

"You see what I mean? 'Laid my heart bare' is a

dreadful cliché. You must learn to avoid trite phrases like that if you're going to write anything worthwhile. Now, as for my being despicable and heartless, let me point out, little cousin, that I didn't run away from you. You deserted me, after writing in your note that you had fallen in love with me. That was a heartless thing for you to do—not to mention completely illogical. You made me very angry, little cousin."

"So that's why you didn't call me at the motel or try to see me before I left. You were sulking!"

"I don't *sulk*," he said acidly. "No, I simply allowed you to go on and play your little game and get it out of your system. One has to be patient with children."

She drew a slow breath, forcing herself to remain as calm as possible under the circumstances. In a voice that surprised her with its steadiness, she replied, "I know you're up to your old tricks, Clement Vaulkhurst, trying to infuriate me so I'll get completely rattled. Well, it won't work. I'm wise to you, 'cousin.' Now, do you want to tell me why you called, or do you just want to go on wasting the expense of a long-distance phone call?"

She heard a low chuckle at the other end of the wire. Then he said, "Very well, I'll tell you why I called. I wanted to see if you're through playing childish games and are ready to come back to me. I must fly to the West Coast next week. Some silly business about a screen adaptation of my book. We're going to see if we can keep Hollywood from totally mutilating what I've written—a rather futile hope, I'm sure. At any rate, I thought it would be an opportune time for us to have a reunion. You could meet me in Houston, and we could fly from there. After we finish with the mundane chore in Hollywood, we could rent a car and motor up the coast to Sausalito, where I have some artist friends. . . ."

Again Deborah felt the wild racing of her pulse. A tremulous bubble of happiness was daring to grow in her heart. But, knowing Clement, she fought to keep her rising excitement under control. "Then," she choked, "you've changed your mind? About marriage, I mean . . ."

"Marriage?" he said blankly.

There was a silence while the bubble of happiness in Deborah slowly deflated. "By 'coming back to you,' I guess you mean on your terms."

"Don't tell me," he said angrily, "you are still going to throw your middle-class conventionality up to me?"

"I think," she said quietly, "in this case, you're confusing conventionality with decency."

"I'm not confused," he said coldly. "Not in the slightest. I can see which one of us is the cold-blooded merchant here. I have a deep feeling for you, a need as old as the human race for us to be together. But you have with great shrewdness put a price tag on your virginity. You are up for sale—and the price is a marriage license and wedding ring!"

Her face was burning with anger and humiliation. "Perhaps, to your bohemian mind, that sounds terribly prudish, old-fashioned, and even conniving. I'm sorry, Clement, but I'm not the kind of woman who can settle for a weekend in Hollywood or a trip to Sausalito, or even a year's cruise around the world. There's something else as old as the human race: some women prefer to save themselves for the man they're going to spend their life with. I'm that kind of woman, and that is the choice I've made. And . . . and if you really cared for me, you'd want it that way, too! But I don't think you love me at all. I don't think you know what love is. You've decided it would be fun to have me in bed with you. You told me once, yourself, that a man can derive a good deal of pleasure out of corrupting and teaching an inexperienced young woman all about the ways of love. That's really all you want me for, and once you've satisfied that desire, I can pack my suitcase and go back home!"

"And I suppose that stuffy, totally unimaginative lawyer boyfriend of yours is quite willing to accept all your conditions of a conventional marriage complete with bridesmaids, a Sara Lee wedding cake, and a first and second mortgage on a vine-covered cottage."

"As a matter of fact, he is," she said. And then, stung deeply, on an angry impulse she blurted out, "You might be interested to know that Bill and I are going to formally announce our engagement at a university faculty party this weekend!"

"Fine!" he raged. "The two of you deserve each other!"

With that, he hung up on her.

Deborah slammed down her telephone. The torrent of tears that followed came from a mixture of anger and heartbreak. "How can I let a man like that do this to me?" she sobbed. Clement Vaulkhurst, she told herself, was a contemptible cad. Yet he was able to break her heart.

"Well, no more!" she thought aloud. She was going to erase Clement from her life once and for all. She was going to forever burn her bridges behind her. "And I don't care if that is a cliché, Clement Vaulkhurst!" she said aloud.

With trembling fingers, she dialed the number of Bill

Hughbank's apartment in New York. When she got him on the phone, Deborah demanded, "Bill, I have to see you. It's very important. Can you drive up here tomorrow night?"

"Tomorrow night? On a Wednesday?" Bill asked, sounding totally confused.

"Yes. Tomorrow night. After you leave your office. It's important," she repeated.

"Well, I don't know. Is something the matter? Can we talk about it on the phone?"

"No, it's not something we can discuss on the phone. I need to see you, Bill. We have to talk."

"Well, you know how the traffic is on a weeknight after work," he began.

The upsetting dialogue she'd had with Clement Vaulkhurst had left her in no mood to debate the matter. "Bill, for once, do something that's not listed on your schedule," she said with exasperation. "I have to talk to you. Are you coming or not?"

"If it's all that important . . ."

"Yes, it is. I'll expect you here by eight or nine." She hung up without giving him the opportunity to object.

Bill arrived shortly after eight o'clock the following night. Deborah, who had been waiting beside a window, ran out to his car. She slid in beside him, a trifle breathlessly, and said, "Drive someplace where we can talk in private."

"Where do you want to go?" he asked, sounding as confused as he had on the telephone.

"For heaven's sake, Bill, you never had any trouble finding a place to park when you wanted to neck!"

"Oh," he said. He turned the car down a drive and in

a short while parked in a secluded spot near the lake that bordered the campus.

He made a move to kiss her, but Deborah pushed him away. "Not now, Bill. We have to get something settled. I want you to tell me honestly how you feel about our getting married."

He blinked at her, struggling to get a grip on this situation she had brought about. "I want to marry you," he said.

"No, that's the first thing that came to your mind. Bill, we have to do some soul-searching, or we're going to mess up both our lives. You know things haven't been the same between us since we came back from Uromund."

"I know," he agreed slowly. "But it's because you've changed, Deborah. Sometimes I have trouble understanding you."

"That's what I mean. Bill, you're going to have a responsible position in a respected old law firm. You need a wife who is conventional, dedicated, utterly respectable. That was why you picked me in the first place. You thought I fit all those classifications. But lately I haven't wanted to be as tied down by convention. I got a taste for once of being free from living my life in constant fear of what other people thought of me and my actions, and I like it. Do you think you can live with a wife like that?"

"Well . . ." He was looking confused again.

There was a moment of strained silence. Then he said, slowly, "Everyone expects us to get married. Your parents are happy about it. My parents think you're great. All our friends take it for granted that we'll be married by Christmas. . . ."

"Yes." She sighed. "I sometimes think we're going ahead with it because our getting married seems inevitable and we're resigned to it."

He was frowning. "No, it's perfectly natural for people about to take the big leap to have second thoughts, to be a little scared. Marriage is so permanent—"

She smiled and touched his hand. " 'Marriage is so permanent,' " she repeated. "Yes, that's the one thing we both agree on—maybe the most important." She drew a deep breath. "Bill, what would you say if I told you I want to announce our engagement at the faculty party this weekend?"

There was a surprised silence. He frowned as he pondered her question. "That seems kind of sudden, doesn't it? I mean, we haven't picked out the engagement ring or anything, yet."

"I know. But it's important to me to make the announcement now."

Yes, important, so I won't give in to temptation to throw my life away if Clement Vaulkhurst calls me again and catches me in a weak moment. . . .

"You don't think we should wait a little longer?" Bill asked.

"Bill, I asked you to be honest. I'll be honest, too. I do have a bad case of jitters about the wedding—just as you do. But getting engaged isn't being married. Why don't we see how we feel after we're engaged? Why don't we announce our engagement, and then wait for a while before setting a definite wedding date? An engagement can always be broken if we see it isn't going to work out."

Bill looked relieved. "Yes, that's a sensible idea."

At the faculty reception that weekend in her parents' home, Deborah couldn't help but be reminded of a similar reception last spring just before she had embarked on her trip to Uromund. There was the same assemblage of university faculty types, the intense, bearded young Ph.D.'s, older professors looking somewhat bored and seedy in tweed jackets, a sprinkling of females, some looking vague and a bit unkempt, self-consciously holding cocktail glasses and cigarettes, others bright and voluble.

Deborah and Bill had not yet made their engagement announcement. She planned to do that midway through the evening. Meanwhile, she was helping her parents greet the guests and seeing that the supply of hors d'oeuvres and drinks was plentiful. She maintained a bright, cheerful smile, stubbornly determined not to admit to herself that her heart was breaking. Clement is out of my life forever, she told herself firmly. I'm not going to spend the rest of my days moping over him. He isn't worth it. I'm going to be engaged to Bill, and I'm going to start a whole new life. I'm going to remember Clement Vaulkhurst as a bad dream that brought me nothing but misery! At least that was what she told herself.

She touched Bill's hand as she moved past him in the crowded room. Her mother was in the center of one conversation group. In another corner of the room, her father was telling a circle of colleagues about his discoveries in the Mayan ruins he had explored this past summer.

Deborah went to the kitchen for a supply of glasses. She was interrupted by her mother, who came into the room, wearing a peculiar expression.

"Is something wrong, Mother?" Deborah asked anxiously. "You look pale."

"Do I?" Dr. Denhoff said absently.

"Yes, you do. What is it, for heaven's sake? Don't you feel all right?"

"Well . . . there's a bit of a problem. I don't exactly know what to do about it. And I don't know what you're going to think of the situation. I mean, I can't exactly have him thrown out, though it is upsetting, his suddenly walking in unannounced. Just like him to pull something like this, of course—"

"Mother," Deborah said exasperatedly, "please stop being incoherent. What are you talking about? *Who* are you talking about?"

Her mother nervously fiddled with her hearing aid. "Clement," she said. "Can you imagine? Suddenly showing up here like this? He just walked in the front door—"

Dimly, Deborah heard a crash at her feet. She was not aware that she'd dropped a glass she had been holding. Her heart seemed to suspend beating. All of her senses rushed together, became blurred, then distinct again. She drew a slow, deep breath, realizing that her hands were clenched so tightly that her knuckles were white. "Clement Vaulkhurst is here, in our house?" she asked in a stranger's voice.

"Yes. Just came barging in. Of course, he *is* a relative, and a most distinguished one at that. But he's so unpredictable. Some of the people from the English department recognized him and it's causing quite a stir. I'm on pins and needles about what Clement will say to them. He's good at insulting people. Your father never had any use for him. I'm afraid they're going to have a run-in. And Bill looks angry. I think you'd better go out there, Deborah. He's demanding to see you."

As Deborah started to the kitchen door, her mother touched her arm. "I—I don't know what happened between you and Clement in Uromund. You're an adult, and I decided it was none of my business. But if it was something unpleasant . . . I mean, if you'd rather not see him—"

Deborah shook her head. She hurried out the kitchen door, almost colliding with Bill. He wore a tight-lipped, angry expression. "Deborah—"

But she was looking past him at a tall figure that dominated the room. She suddenly recalled the electrical storm that had frightened her so badly in the swamp when lightning was crashing into trees all around her. She became aware of the same electric charge in the air. The small hairs on the nape of her neck prickled. She could hear Clement's rumbling baritone over the rushing pound of blood in her ears.

The entire room was focused on the famous novelist. Some of the young, bearded types were gaping at him with openmouthed awe. Others were fawning over him.

"Mr. Vaulkhurst," she heard a woman English professor gush breathlessly, "I teach a creative writing class. What advice could you give my students?"

Clement gave her a withering glance. "Madam," he said, "I would advise them to stop wasting their time with your creative writing class and take up selling real estate. There's more money in it."

Then he spied Deborah. His black-eyed gaze drilled fiercely into her eyes, draining the strength from her legs. Impatiently, he moved the faculty members aside and strode up to her. "I want to talk to you," he thundered.

She swallowed hard. "All—all right."

He glared around them. "Someplace away from these mewing sycophants. Someplace private."

"I had forgotten how abrasive you could be," she said, some of her old anger at him returning. "All right . . . in here." She led him toward a doorway. She was aware of her father's look of annoyance. Bill came up to them, looking belligerent. She said, "Bill, I just want to talk to Clement quietly for a few minutes."

"But—"

She put her hand on his arm. "Please—for my parents' sake, Bill, don't make a scene."

The two men glared at each other, but finally Bill relaxed and nodded reluctantly. "I'll be right here. If you need me, just call."

Deborah hurried Clement into a deserted hallway and closed the door behind them. Through the closed doorway, she could hear the excited murmur of voices in the room they had left.

"What does he mean—if you need him, just call?" Clement demanded. "Does he think I'm going to violate you?"

"Perhaps. Bill is very protective."

Now that she'd survived the first shock, she was able to raise her chin and meet his eyes with icy composure. "Now, just why have you come here, crashing my parents' party, causing a scene?"

"In our telephone conversation this week, you threatened to announce your engagement to that ridiculous kid who has been hanging around you. I couldn't believe you were serious. However, on the possibility that you have taken leave of your senses altogether and actually plan to go through with it, I wanted to come and see for myself."

"I am quite serious," she said coldly. "And totally sane and in command of my senses. If you wish to be present when I make the announcement, come along. I'll do it right now."

She started to the door, but his hand on her arm stopped her.

"I told you a long time ago you have no business marrying that stuffed-shirt lawyer."

"You have no right to tell me who I can or cannot marry!" she gasped.

"You don't love him," Clement said flatly.

She retorted angrily, "That is no business of yours, Clement Vaulkhurst. Bill is a decent man who wants to marry me. You wanted nothing from me but an illicit affair."

"Now you're sounding as stuffy as he is. 'Illicit affair.' Where did you get that phrase—from a soap opera?"

"What else do you call it? You invited me to move into your bedroom, to spend the next year as your traveling companion and bedmate, nothing more. I made it quite clear in the letter I left you that I cannot sleep with a man under those circumstances no matter how much I—I care for him."

"Yes, you were quite explicit in your letter. Didn't have the courage to tell me in person, did you?"

"No," she admitted. "I—I was afraid I might weaken."

"Because you're in love with me, not this Bill whatever-his-name-is," he added, his gaze fierce and penetrating.

She met his eyes bravely. "Yes," she admitted more

softly. "I told you that in my letter. But it doesn't change anything. Even though I loved you, I couldn't sleep with you on your terms. When you made no move to stop me from leaving Uromund, you made it clear that you had no intention of marrying me . . . that all you wanted was a temporary affair."

Clement began pacing back and forth in the confines of the hallway. His giant figure made the room smaller. "Well, I was peeved at you, turning me down that way," he muttered. "Piqued my ego. It appeared to me you were putting stuffy convention above what we felt for each other."

"Clement," she said, "I know you live life on your own terms, make your own rules, and too bad with what others think of you. Up to a point that's very admirable. It's one of the things that attracted me to you—something that has been lacking in my own life. But when it comes to giving myself totally to a man, I still want to live by the rules I've known all my life, the rules that hold our civilization together. I can surrender only to a man who really loves me, who will tell the world he's going to protect me and care for me all my life by putting a wedding ring on my finger—a man who wants to be the father of my children."

He stopped pacing and stood before her, holding her lightly, gazing somberly into her eyes. "I do love you, you know. Have loved you, I think, from the first moment I laid eyes on you."

A sob caught at her throat. "Then why didn't you ever tell me? You just seemed to do all you could to make me angry with you."

"I wanted to make you angry," he explained. "I goaded and taunted you because I wanted you to learn to stand up for yourself, to discover who you are and become an independent adult. I knew you could never be happy with me unless you could learn to live my kind of life, which meant living life on your own terms and not worrying about what others thought of you. By keeping you furious at me much of the time, I think I succeeded in bringing out the potential that has been stifled in you most of your life."

"Yes," she admitted. "I realize you did that, and I'll be forever grateful. But," she said tearfully, "if you really did love me, why didn't you say so? You can't know how much I longed for you to say it."

"Well, I'm saying it now. Perhaps I needed the jolt of this engagement announcement to make me realize I really do love you. To be truthful, I didn't think you'd go this far. I kept believing that in time you'd come crawling back to Uromund, contrite and willing for me to take you in again. Turns out I was wrong. You can be even more stubborn than I!"

He looked at her in a teasing manner. "Since it started by my finding you on my doorstep one night, I don't know if I should adopt you or marry you. However, since it's marriage you want, then it's fine with me."

She turned away from him. "It's too late now," she said, a catch in her voice. "I'm marrying Bill. You can't just barge in here like this at the last minute and try to confuse me." She was crying now, angry and hurt.

"Oh, yes, I can, and I will," he said. Firmly, he turned her to face him. He held her close, and then he kissed her. She tried to struggle out of his arms, but her struggles grew weaker as she realized how desperately hungry she had been for the strength of his arms around her, his magic touch making her alive and tingling all over again. That part of her that had been a traitor to her common sense from the beginning took control again and responded passionately to his kiss.

Then he said, "Now, if you dare go through with this ridiculous marriage to Bill whatsis, I'll break up the wedding by riding a horse into the church. I'll show up with a fake marriage license and swear you and I were married in Mexico. . . ."

She looked at him helplessly. "You'd do it, too, wouldn't you? It would appeal to your sense of the dramatic!"

"Sure, I'd do that and worse to keep you. Deborah, you have taught me that certain conventions such as a marriage license deserve my respect. Perhaps we learned some things from each other. I do want to marry you, little cousin, very much. I came here to marry you."

From his pocket he took a velvet case and opened it to show her a set of rings, a diamond in a simple yellow-gold setting and a gold wedding band. "They belonged to my foster mother, your Aunt Christina. She sends them with her blessing."

Tears trickled down Deborah's cheeks. "What can I say?" she whispered. "I do love you. I have no control where you are concerned. I do want very much to be your wife, Clement. . . ."

"How about Bill whatever-his-name-is?"

"Hughbank."

"Whatever. How about him?"

She sighed. "I think I'll be doing poor Bill a favor. He'll be relieved once he recovers from the shock. He hasn't been comfortable with me ever since I came back from Uromund. He keeps hoping that I'll revert to the little mouse he used to know—but I'm sure I never will. I think Bill was resigned to going through with the wedding, perhaps through some sense of duty or obligation to me, but I know his heart hasn't been in it. I really twisted the poor guy's arm into making the announcement tonight. So . . . we're not doing anything to hurt Bill. He'll really be much happier with someone else."

"But how about your parents, your friends, the school faculty? There will be a bit of a scandal, your changing your mind at the last minute this way."

She shook her head. "My life is too important to be bound by what other people think or say about me. You taught me that."

He tucked her arm in his. "Very well, let's go back in and liven up the party. It's obviously been a deadly bore up to now. Your father will want to throw me out on my ear. Bill Hughbank will want to poke me in the jaw. And in the midst of it all, the whole English department will be pulling on my coattails, wanting my autograph. Should turn out to be one whale of an evening."

She grinned at him. "And you're going to relish it, Clement Vaulkhurst!" She had the feeling that from now on her life would never know a boring moment.

Silhouette **Romance**

15-Day Free Trial Offer
6 Silhouette Romances

6 Silhouette Romances, free for 15 days! We'll send you 6 new Silhouette Romances to keep for 15 days, absolutely free! If you decide not to keep them, send them back to us. We'll pay the return postage. You pay nothing.

Free Home Delivery. But if you enjoy them as much as we think you will, keep them by paying us the retail price of just $1.50 each. We'll pay all shipping and handling charges. You'll then automatically become a member of the Silhouette Book Club, and will receive 6 more new Silhouette Romances every month and a bill for $9.00. That's the same price you'd pay in the store, but you get the convenience of home delivery.

Read every book we publish. The Silhouette Book Club is the way to make sure you'll be able to receive every new romance we publish.

This offer expires October 31, 1981

Silhouette Romance

ROMANCE THE WAY
IT USED TO BE...
AND COULD BE AGAIN

Contemporary romances for today's women.

Each month, six very special love stories will be yours

from SILHOUETTE.

Look for them wherever books are sold

or order now from the coupon below.

$1.50 each

Silhouette Romance

____ #49 DANCER IN THE SHADOWS Wisdom
____ #50 DUSKY ROSE Scott
____ #51 BRIDE OF THE SUN Hunter
____ #52 MAN WITHOUT A HEART Hampson
____ #53 CHANCE TOMORROW Browning
____ #54 LOUISIANA LADY Beckman
____ #55 WINTER'S HEART Ladame
____ #56 RISING STAR Trent
____ #57 TO TRUST TOMORROW John
____ #58 LONG WINTER'S NIGHT Stanford
____ #59 KISSED BY MOONLIGHT Vernon
____ #60 GREEN PARADISE Hill
____ #61 WHISPER MY NAME Michaels
____ #62 STAND-IN BRIDE Halston

____ #63 SNOWFLAKES IN THE SUN Brent
____ #64 SHADOW OF APOLLO Hampson
____ #65 A TOUCH OF MAGIC Hunter
____ #66 PROMISES FROM THE PAST Vitek
____ #67 ISLAND CONQUEST Hastings
____ #68 THE MARRIAGE BARGAIN Scott
____ #69 WEST OF THE MOON St. George
____ #70 MADE FOR EACH OTHER Afton Bonds
____ #71 A SECOND CHANCE ON LOVE Ripy
____ #72 ANGRY LOVER Beckman
____ #73 WREN OF PARADISE Browning
____ #74 WINTER DREAMS Trent
____ #75 DIVIDE THE WIND Carroll

Coming in June From Silhouette

JANET DAILEY'S
THE HOSTAGE BRIDE

- - - - - - - - - - - - - - - - - - - -

SILHOUETTE BOOKS. Department SB/1
1230 Avenue of the Americas
New York, NY 10020

Please send me the books I have checked above. I am enclosing
$_____ (please add 50¢ to cover postage and handling. NYS and
NYC residents please add appropriate sales tax). Send check or
money order—no cash or C.O.D.'s please. Allow six weeks for delivery.

NAME_____

ADDRESS_____

CITY_____STATE/ZIP_____